Praise for *Beyond the Comma*

A clear and clarion call for building a ju
from deep religious pathos, Chase's ge
needed charge leading us in the footste
raises all the crucial questions and answers with bold exclamation points!

—Rabbi Naamah Kelman
Dean of Hebrew Union College, the Reform Seminary in Jerusalem

Life's most precious gems of wisdom may be missed because we are too
hurried to stop, look and listen at points of interruption or delay. Chase's rich
treasury of insights and observations makes a convincing case that we must
value more highly than ever before God's gifts of pauses and punctuations
along our pilgrimage of life.

—The Rev. Dr. James Forbes
former Senior Minister, The Riverside Church, New York City

Robert Chase weaves stories, theological reflection, and a passion for justice
in this book that reveals "intersectionality" as the paradigm for a hopeful future.
He blends the personal, cultural, and religious spheres with honesty and
courage. Bob's compelling moral vision is one that inspires me in these
challenging times. On a day that you need a reason to hope, pick up this book!

—The Rev. Dr. Nancy Wilson
global moderator of Metropolitan Community Church

Based in compassion and moral courage, Rev. Chase offers hope and guidance
in these times marred by religious and ethnic conflicts. We owe him a debt of
gratitude for sharing his profound and learned reflections with us.

—Ambassador Akbar Ahmed
Ibn Khaldun Chair of Islamic Studies, American University, Washington, D.C.

Bob Chase reminds us there are moments in life when we need to step back and consider the important things that define the path forward. Here is a roadmap on how to choose the right forks in the road.

As a professed agnostic, I've often looked upon Christianity—and all organized religions—with skepticism and mistrust. Reverend Chase has worked to create a different example of Christianity—an inclusive, nonjudgmental faith that brings people of different paths together at the intersections of life. *Beyond the Comma* is an exploration of those moments when the forces that guide us prompt self-examination and a deeper journey to discover our place in the world.

BEYOND

THE

COMMA

Beyond the Comma

Life at the Intersection

Robert Chase

The Pilgrim Press
Cleveland

TO | *my parents,*

Bob and Arlene Chase,

without whose nurturing

love I would be but a

shadow of who I am

The Pilgrim Press, 700 Prospect Avenue, Cleveland, Ohio 44115
thepilgrimpress.com
©2017 by Robert Chase

Printed in the United States of America on acid-free paper

19   18   17   16   15   5   4   3   2   1

ISBN: 978-0-8298-2043-0

CONTENTS

Acknowledgments

Writing is a solitary pursuit. Producing a book for public consumption is anything but. There are so many people to thank who supported me in this task. I begin with my parents, to whom this book is dedicated. Without their selfless love, I would not have had the emotional foundation to put my thoughts on paper and share them with the world.

I am grateful to my four "early readers," Gwen Crider, Hans Holznagel, Tim Crist, and Melody Fox Ahmed. Respected colleagues from various times in my life, they read a first draft of the opening pages of my manuscript and declared the project worth pursuing, encouraging me to write with confidence because my voice was valid and valuable.

I want to thank the Governing Board and the dedicated staff at Intersections, who demonstrated patience and forbearance in allowing me the time and energy needed to complete this task.

I am especially grateful to my editor and long-time friend and colleague, Betsy McHaley. Without her critical eye and gentle prodding, the result would have been less successful and the exercise far less enjoyable. I offer a special thanks to my assistant Michael McKee, who filled in so many gaps in the process; to Dr. Michael Brown and his gracious staff at Marble Collegiate Church, who provided space to complete this manuscript, allowing me a place of consistent respite as the world swirled around me; and to Tina Villa and her team at the Pilgrim Press, willing to take a risk on this untried writer.

I am deeply grateful to those whose lives intersected mine—sometimes for a brief moment, sometimes for a lifetime—providing both "comma moments" and life-altering intersections.

And, finally, I am grateful to my wife, Blythe, who has been quietly supportive in so many ways, large and small. Without her love and companionship, I would never have had the courage to undertake this task.

Thank you, all. Bob

Prologue

You may never have proof of your importance,
but you are more important than you think.
There are always those who couldn't do without you.
The rub is that you don't always know who.[1]

—*Robert Fulghum*

Remember the nursery rhyme to promote safety in the streets? "Cross at the green and not in between." That childish strophe is a starting point for the pages that follow. Its lesson draws you to the intersection where the traffic light is found but also where, as I hope these pages will reveal, there is so much more. True, intersections have rules, both formal and informal, that order oncoming traffic flow. We can become captive by these rules, allowing us to stagnate; or the rules of the road can free us to become more than we could ever have hoped or imagined.[2]

A friend of mine, Arvind Vora, is chair for Interreligious Affairs of the Federation of Jain Associations in North America and a traffic engineer by profession. He reports that when two vehicles enter an intersection, there are *sixteen* possible safe interactions. It is pursuit of these options (and imagining others) that is core to the narrative that follows. At the intersection, we can discover one another and find that life can shift in wholly unanticipated directions. "Behold," says God, "I am about to do a new thing; now it springs forth, do you not see it?" (Isa. 43:19).

I have become increasingly aware of the simultaneous intersections that confront us in each moment. In vulnerable times, the confluence of these forces can seem overwhelming. In ordinary times, the tendency is to overlook or ignore these competing dynamics and live one-dimensionally. But if we are to be truly attentive to the seemingly contradictory realities that compete for our attention, existence can be enriched, understanding deepened, and options expanded in limitless ways.

Walt Disney built an empire based on two such seemingly conflicting ideas: memory—which looks to the past—and imagination—which builds on an illimitable future.[3] When brought into harmony, the deep tap root of past experience merges with an open-ended future inspired by creativity and invention. By making decisions based on both past and future—memory *and* imagination—the present is expanded exponentially. By the same token, if we live in touch with both our deeply personal realities, while at the same time engaging the global forces that surround us, our sensitivities are heightened and our potential for becoming more creative, sensitive, and productive is enhanced.

What are best practices in navigating such a convergent reality? How do we learn from the life experiences that cascade across our individual emotional, spiritual, and intellectual countenance while remaining attuned to societal issues that surround us? Are there lessons to be learned from the varied forces that bombard our senses? Are there even deeper lessons to be learned about the cosmos by comparing and contrasting the marker that is our particular lifespan with the longer arc of history?

The purpose of this book is twofold: to lift up the awareness of these forces that are constantly at work on all of us, all of the time; and to explore ways of creatively engaging this dynamic in order to enrich our lives, achieve our aspirations, and enhance our sense of fulfillment. The concept of "intersection" as a multilayered prism for self-discovery can lead to increased understanding of self, our world, and the human condition.

On a personal level, events from half a century ago when I was quite young, when examined through the refraction of multiple experiences over time, reveal remarkably similar lessons. How are these things related? How can I make decisions *now* that build upon lessons learned *then*? Are there organizational principles that we can use to heighten positive possibilities while avoiding unnecessary pain? Can we avoid missed opportunities that continue to keep us in bondage: to traditions, to patterns of behavior, to limited views of the world and the magnificent mosaic of our global village?

These writings do not fit neatly into categories. They do not represent a business plan or a personal guide to self-improvement. Nor are they a series of parables or morality tales. Muriel Rukeyser reminds us that the universe is made up of stories, not atoms,[4] and there are many stories in this narrative. All, I hope, serve to portray the mosaic that is life itself—yours, mine, others. At the time of this writing, I was serving as founding director of Intersections International, a nonprofit organization dedicated to bringing individuals, communities, and whole nations together to promote justice and peace. Our task is often to connect the dots, and so it is with this narrative—offering you, the reader, an opportunity to make the seemingly disparate connections in your own life, so that you can discover anew what Dr. Martin Luther King calls the interrelated structure of reality.[5]

The whole exercise of writing a book implies that you think you have something important to say, and others will want to read it. The fear is that you discover your thoughts are too simplistic, too pedestrian, or too obtuse to be of interest to anyone. This is especially true for me since my life— while full and for which I am grateful—has not seemed particularly remarkable or dramatic or beneficent or filled with self-sacrifice. I am a product

In moments of doubt and disillusionment, I ask, "What do I have to say that could be of value?"

of the suburbs—how unimaginative. I'm a white, male Christian of privilege—no drama there. I have been spared the gut-wrenching tragedies that so often infuse the lives of others who have truly heroic stories to tell. I never went to war or ran for office and never led a movement of any real consequence. And, so I ask myself in those moments of doubt and disillusionment, what do I have to say that could be of value?

I'm reminded of a sermon I once heard, "Between Terror and Amazement," about the discovery of the women at the tomb on the first Easter. They were both terrified and amazed by what they saw.[6] Ah, yet another intersection. This biblical passage sets a perfect context for the underlying premise of this book and begs the question about what it means to be *fully* human. In Genesis we learn that we've been created in the image and likeness of the Creator God. We have been given both the ability and the desire to "make things." We've been endowed with both memory *and* imagination and we have both the privilege *and* the responsibility to be co-creators with God. But this prospect also terrifies us because the outcome is so uncertain and, as human beings, we fear uncertainty and cling relentlessly to the status quo.

I ask, "Is it not in just those moments, between terror and amazement, where so many of us live?" So, putting aside doubts and fears, I wonder if I am not *exactly* the one who should write such a book. Perhaps, if I see myself as painfully normal and then try to extract life lessons from my experience, this will resonate with those who, like me, wonder about who they are and why they are here. I have come across many moments when I thought it would be a good and productive thing to document thoughts and ideas about these intersections in my life. In the following pages, you can see—and judge for yourself—the value of this exercise.

1 | Gratitude

i thank You God for most this amazing

day . . . for everything

which is natural which is infinite which is yes[1]

—e. e. cummings

Along with the profoundly inventive poet e. e. cummings, we begin with gratitude: for this world, this life, this moment, for all those whose paths cross ours, whom we are privileged to engage in our lives, and for the opportunities to meet extraordinary challenges by doing amazing things. This is the starting point for integration of all that has come to pass with all that is yet to be. If this overarching understanding remains constant, infinite possibilities abound, and for that I begin with, "i thank You God."

It has been my life's calling to create intersections, not boundaries, among those who differ. What prompted this call? What shaped the prin-

ciples upon which my life's work is based? How can the confluence of
forces in my own life be inspirational and instructive for others?

As founding director of Intersections International, a multifaith, multicultural initiative of the Collegiate Church of New York, I am engaged with
individuals and communities at those "thin places" where conflicts, misunderstandings, stereotyping, and even violence can occur. These places include the "intersections" of power and values, faith and science, memory
and hope, imagination and action, life and death, order and chaos, sacred
and secular, male and female, war and peace, present and future, doubt and
belief—because it is in such places that the most cosmic of all questions
are asked: Who am I? Why am I here? And, for people of faith: Does God
care about my life?

There are many points where I could begin these reflections, but perhaps a good place to start is in Islamabad, in a room surrounded by two
hundred Pakistanis—men in long beards and traditional dress, women in
chadors and hijabs. The vast majority had never met an American. I was
there to explore bringing an interfaith group of U.S. religious leaders to Pakistan to be in dialogue with Pakistani counterparts, and I was addressing a
group on the campus of the International Islamic University as to why I
thought this was a good idea. Someone rose from the crowd and declared,
"I know that your Holy Scripture [John 14:6] says that Jesus is the only way
and that no one comes to the father except through him. Christians believe
that Muslims are going to hell. At best, you are not here to talk to us. You
just want to convert us."

How was I to respond? Though I pride myself on being liberal (as Bob
Dylan writes, "but to a degree"), I was clearly a stranger in a strange land. In
a bit, I will return to how I *actually* responded, but to fully answer the question, I need to go way back to a time in my childhood when I first realized
that I was different—no, not so different that I'd never be able to blend in
(why do kids so desperately want to "blend in"?), but different enough.

I guess you could say the story began in second grade. It was a day, as I
recall, like any other, but it would start a series of innocuous events that

would conspire together to awaken in me a knowledge that I would not be the fully complete human being—at least in a physical sense—that my doting parents had always assured me I could be and that community leaders—teachers, pastors, counselors—implied was my right. The very premise may have been unrealistic and was certainly based upon what I would much later come to know as "privilege." Still, such parental encouragement, with its societal support, shaped my early years with the idea that anything was possible.

I was called to the nurse's office for a routine eye exam. I don't really remember what she said, but when I gave my mother the note from the nurse, it was clear that I needed glasses. With sixty years' perspective, this seems like a rather minor wrinkle, but in my seven-year-old consciousness, it was devastating. Glasses! From that time forward, I would have to wear glasses to be able to see properly. I remember my uncle telling me jovially at the time that every day his glasses were the first thing he put on in the morning and the last thing he took off at night. He was trying to be reassuring, but actually it sounded like a curse—a trap that would forever ensnare me in a routine—every day! I know, I thought, I will rebel. I will not go quietly into the cold, dark night!

The first thing I noticed when I got my new glasses was that you could see individual leaves on the trees. Now that was pretty cool. For me, trees had always appeared as mottled green blurs, not unlike an impressionistic painting. To see the distinctions in branches and leaves was pretty extraordinary. But such benefits did not outweigh the stigma of having to wear glasses—always to be a nerd (even though the term "nerd" wasn't invented yet), and, so I feared, be excluded from the in-crowd. So, for my rebellious act: every day for the next two years, I dutifully put my glasses into their case, put the case in my pocket, and took my glasses to school. But I never wore them, never even let anyone see them. For two years.

I learned to cope. When the teacher routinely switched our seats, moving me to the back of the class, I realized I couldn't see the flashcards that she used to drill us in arithmetic. So I memorized the order of the cards on their shiny metal ring. I breezed through them, confidently calling out the problems—"six times eight equals forty-eight"—even though I couldn't see a thing! It was a survival technique, a way I could avoid being different.

One night, my folks invited a friend over for dinner. Phil Sheridan was his name. My favorite television program was on after dinner. TV was a relatively new phenomenon—Phil didn't have one—and my Mom thought it would be great for Phil and me to watch our new television together. "No!" my insides screamed, "We can't watch television together! Phil would see my glasses!" And my folks would be suspicious if I didn't wear them, so I threw a tantrum trying to keep Phil from coming to dinner. I couldn't say why and made up all sorts of ridiculous excuses for him to stay away. I finally relented and confessed, acknowledging two years' worth of deception. My infinitely patient mother declared it no big deal (she was right, of course) and I decided to watch the show with my glasses. It was also no big deal to Phil. He hardly seemed to notice. The next day I went to school wearing those glasses and I have worn corrective lenses every day since.

A life lesson was unfolding without my even realizing it, and yet what innocently occurred in that living room in Levittown, New York, began to form a fundamental principle for my adult interactions. As someone later said in a much different context, "You're different, dude. Get over it."

You're different. Get over it.

Actually, we're all different and it is precisely in our differences that life's magnificent mosaic is revealed. I listened to Phil. What was, for me, a very big deal —wearing glasses—was inconsequential to him. By realizing his total lack of concern and then shifting my actions accordingly, my life changed. Harkening back to the Robert Fulghum's classic *All I Really Need to Know I Learned in Kindergarten* I now recognize that a vital principle in constructive human interaction—listen to the unexpected—I first experienced, perhaps not in kindergarten, but before my tenth birthday. And those unexpected lessons from surprising sources mark a core tenet in my life's story and in this narrative.

The poignant epilogue to this story occurred more than a dozen years later. I heard the news, mixed in with a thousand other stories large and small, that Phil

Listen to the unexpected.

Sheridan had been killed in Vietnam. I never told him about the drama in my life in which he played such a central part. It was so trivial compared to the ultimate sacrifice he had made (for me) and I was sad that I had never been able to share the story with him. I thought he'd get a real chuckle out of it, and that maybe he'd be able to see in the humor the valuable lesson I had learned from him and how it would shape my future.

I have wondered what prompts me to begin this book here. The journey of this narrative generally concerns the movement from fear to empathy, from ignorance to understanding, and from apathy to action. It is about self-discovery in an age fraught with division, isolation, insecurity, hopelessness, violence, and fear—elements so overwhelmingly consequential that it almost seems a sacrilege to start with such a small incident as the first time I wore glasses. Why start here? And why do I connect this very personal story with Vietnam—something so potent, with such a lasting imprint on the human psyche that memories of and reactions to the Vietnam War factored directly into the presidential campaigns throughout the twentieth and into the early twenty-first century, more than fifty years after the war was fought?

But I have come to realize that it is by connecting seemingly opposite poles—intensely personal, and even mundane, experiences with historical events that touch countless lives—that I have discovered a central lesson about what it means to be fully human. As individuals, we intersect with both personal and corporate realities, and we are challenged to integrate our lifestyles and perspectives in ways that include both and ignore neither. It is not sufficient to be consistent and faithful in one context and arbitrary and unforgiving in the other. So starting with a silly personal story about my youthful hang-up over wearing glasses and connecting this to the much wider reality of Vietnam marks an important passage into what it means to live at the many simultaneous intersections that envelope us.

So, back in Islamabad, how was I to respond to my questioner? True, I am a Christian, and the challenge before me had become increasingly relevant in our interrelated world: How do Christians answer the call of exclusivity in the eyes of God? If we believe that Jesus is the *only* way to God, is it not our duty—out of love and compassion for the "other"—to convince those who do not believe in Jesus that he is the singular path to salvation? Are we unfaithful if we do not do this? That moment offered a real-time application of a core tension of my work at Intersections: how can we be both unabashedly multifaith while still being unapologetically Christian?

Given this backdrop, a first step in answering the challenge posed to me in Islamabad lies in the context out of which Intersections was created and in which we do our work. The Collegiate Church of New York, our parent organization, is the oldest corporation in North America, dating back to 1628, whereas Intersections was launched in 2007. Located in a place where God's great mosaic is revealed on any given street corner, down almost any block, Intersections' mandate is to work with communities in conflict and build respectful relationships across lines of difference.

Intersections was created in the wake of a longing throughout our land that we should not be pigeon-holed into neat boxes, clearly defined silos, precise categories, but that the human condition is fluid and we are called to embrace that fluidity in order to achieve our full human potential.

Because the world is fractured and systems of injustice oppress human beings and stifle potential, Intersections exists to harness the power of unlikely voices to speak and act for peace, justice, and reconciliation. We bring together communities in conflict and crisis with our unique and proven ability to convene and spark constructive, open conversations around the issues that divide us. We gather diverse—and often unexpected—voices around a common table. We create safe space for the free flow of ideas. We seek innovative solutions to some of the world's most pressing problems.

We use the arts, traditional media, and emerging technologies to amplify ideas evoked in group dialogue and we initiate concrete, sustainable, ongoing engagements to heal communities over time. We are in the mix, addressing the very "stuff" of life and helping communities navigate the challenges that hinder global human progress. This became a critical juncture for me, where principles and programs converged. In many ways, it marks the culmination of my vocational quest, while addressing God's unfolding reality and exploring ways that my life could "intersect" with world affairs. It is an extraordinary way to experience possibilities "beyond the comma."[2]

Ever New

Life must be lived forwards, but can only be understood backwards.[1]

—Soren Kierkegaard

will never forget my first day on the job as pastor of the Presbyterian Church of Teaneck, New Jersey. I was in my late twenties and filled with visions of the possibilities that serving in this multiracial congregation held for my career. I was excited about the things I would do, the people I would meet, the mark I would make.

But as I approached the church, the minister from the Lutheran Church a block away was also walking to work. He was near retirement and since I was new to town—and, candidly, looked far too young to be the pastor of an established congregation—he did not know who I was. The moment provided an opportunity for me to observe him as he moved slowly along, eyes down, muttering to himself, probably about some nagging issue that was troubling his small congregation. For a fleeting moment, I panicked and asked myself if this was to be my future—to spend my life worrying over the small, petty things that occur in the communities of care we call congregations? Forty years from now, would this be me, moving along a quiet suburban street, stooped over, eyes down, looking lost and burdened by the weight of small things? While I later came to deeply appreciate and respect the amount of work involved in being an effective congregational minister, and the vital role that pastors play in the lives of individuals and families, I decided at that moment that somehow my life would have to be so much more. I did not know how this would happen, but I knew it was essential to my well-being.

So, there I was in Islamabad. Talk about differences!

I was an American in Pakistan seeking to harmonize the discordant notes between our two countries and asking: What makes this distinctly Christian? How do Christians maintain the discreet tenets of our faith while not excluding those who express the concerns raised in that room in the Pakistani capital? When I am confronted by difficult questions, my training as a minister calls on me to turn to Scripture. There, I am reminded how we see evidence of radical shifts occurring right within the text itself and why we are called to be open to such shifts in our own lives.

For example, in Isaiah 43, we read about a qualitatively new thing that God is doing in our midst and that we are challenged to discern how this "new thing" impacts our lives.[2] This portion of Isaiah was written during the final years of the Babylonian Exile. It was not a good time for the Hebrew people. Exile is never a good time. Their culture was threatened, their people disheartened; but the author had great faith in God as intervening in human affairs. A new Exodus would emerge. God would surely restore the Israelites to Judea.

The context of salvation in this passage is found in Israel's memory. God's saving grace doesn't just arise out of nowhere; it has a prototype: the Exodus from Egypt. The image of slavery to freedom through the experience of wilderness wanderings was seared into the consciousness of the people,

> Remember; do not remember—just a single verse apart.

shaping their self-understanding, defining their culture. So, while these verses speak of a new salvation, it is one clearly rooted in the past.

"Remember," implies the prophet, "the Lord makes a way in the sea, a path in the mighty waters and brings out chariot and horse, army and warrior; they lie down, they cannot rise." And so, we are called to remember. But, *in the very next verse*, the prophet proclaims: "Do not remember!" What came before is context, but now is the command: *Do not remember!*

Even the Exodus, the prophet is saying, can be idolized. We can be so fixed in our understanding of it that we fail to realize the new signs of life breaking out all around us, qualitatively new challenges and opportunities that lift us out of our past and cause us to consider our world through a totally new lens.

If Scripture can shift 180 degrees in a single verse, are we not also called to radically rethink deeply ingrained notions every moment? Only by continually taking stock in how we view our world, listening to the unexpected, and operating on the "remember/do not remember" principle in Isaiah 43 can we discover anew what it means to be fully human. Change is inevitable. Even principles that we have believed to be inviolate can change, and if we do not adapt, we may perish.

When the prophet Isaiah implies "remember" and then in the next breath says "do not remember," there is reason to believe that "no one comes to the father, except by me" can live easily alongside a worldview that calls us to be unapologetically Christian while also being unabashedly multifaith.

Sometimes, the most powerful examples of faithfulness are not seen in the lives of those who have been favored, but those who demonstrate faithfulness in the most awful of circumstances, who trust in God despite all evidence to the contrary. I find countless examples, both within and beyond Christianity, of individuals who live simply and in accord with their convictions, who love God and treat neighbors with dignity, compassion, and respect.

I am reminded of a person from the church I served in Teaneck, New Jersey, back in the late 1970s and early '80s. Her name was Eurika Freeman and she suffered from sickle cell anemia, a profoundly painful and debilitating disease that is usually fatal. I visited Eurika often as she became increasingly homebound. Her ten-year-old son also suffered from the disease. In one visit, I mentioned to her that we'd be taking up a canned food collection for the poor the Sunday before Thanksgiving. On the appointed day, people from the congregation came forward down the center aisle in a wave to deposit their canned goods on the communion table, bringing bags and bags of goods. And then as the congregation parted and returned to their seats down the side aisles, there was Eurika Freeman, haltingly making her way forward with her couple of cans of food for those who had less. *A powerful Christian witness.*

I am also reminded of the story told by playwright Kim Schultz in *No Place Called Home,* a theatrical presentation about the plight of Iraqi refugees that Intersections produced in 2009. Playing multiple parts in the drama, Kim portrayed one refugee, Muhammad, who suffered unimaginable humiliation, fear, violence, and dislocation—including finding a human head on his fence post one morning—a head! (This was before the time of ISIS and their horrific executions that often included beheading, so for Western audiences such an image was startling and disturbing beyond words.) Yet, as the playwright recalled, Muhammad always began his story pointedly, "First, I give all thanks to Allah." *A powerful Muslim witness.* And, truth be known, the inspiration for the very opening words of this book.

Always view your life's story within a context of gratitude.

So, my answer in that room in Islamabad revolved around this idea: it is not for me to judge who God considers faithful; my task is to live my life according to how I believe God is calling *me,* while leaving it to others to determine their relationship to God. No, I was not there to judge and I was certainly not there to convert anyone. I was there to listen to the unexpected, to stories I had not yet heard and share my own stories with those I did not yet know.

Listening to the unexpected, discovering a broader picture, is a learned discipline. I gleaned a lot from my high school basketball coach, Don Frisina, who in my senior year guided our team to a sectional championship (the highest level in New York State high school athletics). One of his most important teachings was shared not on the hardwood but behind the wheel of an old sedan with two sets of brakes in the front seat. Coach was also my Drivers' Education instructor—a mandatory class in my day, now relegated to a quaint artifact of ancient history. His advice, as he counseled me to scan the whole windshield: "Get the big picture." This proved invaluable on the road, on the court, and in life itself.

Later, I came to understand that in addition to getting the big picture, it was also necessary to "pay attention to the details." Attending to both elements is necessary if life is to be lived to its fullest. My persistently patient wife, Blythe, is a detail person and is always chastising me for what I miss because I am too focused on "big-picture" thinking, missing many of the pieces of the mosaic that give life its richness.

Attend to both the details and the big picture.

The classic example of this occurred in Amsterdam. Blythe and I were on vacation and, as we were walking through the Centre District, filled with wide-eyed tourists and busy shoppers, we were confronted with a unique advertising campaign for a new video game system. A phalanx of attractive, leggy models danced in formation down the center of a pedestrian thoroughfare, high stepping in military precision to piped-in electronic music. After the cordon of women passed by, I turned to Blythe and exclaimed how cool it was—a formation of models commandeering the whole street, moving in unison to a tune from the new electronic game. Knowing of my attention to big-picture thinking at the expense of the details, Blythe looked at me and asked, "Did you see that they were naked?" Dozens of naked women and I had totally missed it. If our experience is to be comprehensive, in any situation we must engage both broader realities and specific details.

3 Listening

Writing, too, is 90 percent listening. . . .
The deeper you can listen, the better you can write.[1]

—Natalie Goldberg

In the eleventh and tenth century BCE, Israelite tribes formed a loose confederation with no central government. People were led by ad hoc chieftains known as judges. At the end of this era, according to Hebrew Scripture, it was a time when "the word of the LORD was rare in those days" (1 Sam. 3:1). I am reminded of countless laments I hear in our own time, more commonly expressed as, "Where is God in this?" One time this poignant refrain was echoed over and over was in 2014 when we were assaulted by headlines with unusual alacrity—Ebola, ISIS, immigrant children spat upon at the Texas border, Ferguson, Eric Garner, the rapid advance of global warming, a Taliban sniper attack killing 150 children in Pakistan, the murder of two New York City police officers. In December, we prayed for a reprieve in 2015—and then, before the first week of the New Year was over, there was the terrorist attack on the offices of Charlie Hebdo in Paris and the almost unnoticed report of Boko Haram killing two thousand civilians in Nigeria. And so the phrase in 1 Samuel that the word of God was rare in those days took on an all too contemporary ring.

Eli, the next to last of Israel's judges, was aged—both physically and emotionally—from the heartaches brought on by poor decisions of his predecessors and others in positions of leadership. In Judges chapters 17–31, we see Israel devolving into a state of moral demise and ruin, the worship of idols and civil war. "In those days there was no king in Israel; the people did what was right in their own eyes" (Judg. 21:25). Israel was reduced to an anarchic time when those who led the nation exercised a lust for power and greed and a denigration of women, leaving little room for divine pronouncements. Thus begins the story of Samuel, who works for Eli as an apprentice at the Temple.

While in service to Eli, Samuel hears God's voice in the night, prompting him to respond, "Here I am, for you called me" (1 Sam. 3:5). Samuel is still inexperienced and thinks it is Eli, not YHWH (the word for God in Hebrew Scripture), who was speaking. But the older man denies calling Samuel and sends him back to bed.

At first, Eli does not even consider that YHWH would talk to Samuel—young, inexperienced, and of no real standing in the community. But Samuel is persistent. This happens three times. Finally, Eli instructs Samuel to respond, shifting the subject of his response from himself ("Here I am") to God ("Speak, Lord"). Only then does the boy hear God's words. When Samuel suppresses his own voice to hear God's, he gets a spectacular proclamation: "I am about to do something in Israel that will make both ears of anyone who hears of it tingle."

If you enter a conversation with a question, you demonstrate curiosity about "the other." If you then take the time to listen, you can learn all kinds of new things. Once I heard Phil Sheridan's reaction (or lack thereof) to my wearing glasses, I was freed from the supposed trap that visual impairment limited my possibilities. In the Samuel story, this shift in emphasis opens the door for God's call to be heard and then delivered to a people hungry for justice. But God is persistent. Three times Eli's sleep is disturbed. How many times in our day are we asleep to God's word in our midst?

> Switching the subject and the object is a valuable tactic in strategic dialogue.

The lesson from this seems clear, even in our time when we believe "the word of the Lord is rare." If we listen attentively for the sound of God's voice, we will be able to discern it. The message we hear will not always be comforting—Samuel began his prophecy by telling Eli that there would be no mercy for his household because of the things he and his children had done to the people Israel. Yet, Samuel continued to proclaim God's word as he understood it to an often reluctant people.

The phrase "both ears of anyone who hears it tingle" (not just "one" ear, mind you, but both ears—enlisting one's full attention) reminds me of Dr. Martin Luther King Jr.'s great legacy as a preacher, a prophet of nonviolence, and an advocate for justice. The word of God was also "rare" in the time of Martin Luther King, and many of us who lived in that time remember how sleepy we were.

Can we not hear the echo of Samuel or Dr. King in our day? Can we not be stirred to action by the challenges before us? These obstacles seem unique to our time, but are they no less critical than in sixth-century BCE Palestine or 1960s America?

It took me a while to understand that the teachings of the church evolve over time and at any given historical moment there is room for error. It is important to remember that the church is not always right. In 1848, Mrs. Cecil Anderson published *Hymns for Little Children*, which included the hymn "All Things Bright and Beautiful." Those of us of a certain age may well remember that hymn. I sang it in Sunday school. The third verse contains these words:

The rich man in his castle, the poor man at his gate,
God made them, high or lowly, and ordered their estate.[2]

This hymn was used by the church in the nineteenth century as a cudgel against trade unions, because there was fear that union membership would alter the "estates" that God had ordained. Really, now, does God "ordain" social status? If we strive to leave our status behind, are we in jeopardy of working against God's ordination?

Likewise, though I may feel righteous, I am not always right. Yet, even in my fallibility, if I am attentive, the world offers up possibilities for service and satisfaction when we least expect it. One question I am often asked is when I felt called to go to seminary. At least for me, this is not an easy question to answer. There was no lightning bolt, no Damascus Road experience. Rather, it was an emerging sense that evolved over time. I cannot really remember when "both my ears tingled" and I began considering a call to ministry. Yet, if pressed, I can narrow the process to a single pivotal day when I was a junior in college.

I had been attending a new church start in Doylestown, Pennsylvania, under the leadership of Rev. Gordon Dragt, who was to become the single most influential person in my journey into the ministry. The congregation had an inviting, radical worship style, a profound connection to music, theater, and the arts and a deep commitment to social justice. The church was located uncomfortably in suburban Philadelphia where the neighbors were not always happy with the sounds of contemporary music and youthful exuberance that emerged from the small congregation both on Sunday mornings and throughout the week, especially on Saturday night when local teens gathered at the Crossroads Coffee House.

On one particular day, I was ushering at Sunday morning service. As soon as the service began, from the garage next door I heard loud, discordant musical strains blaring through loudspeakers set up in the garage, facing the church. The woman who lived there was definitely not a fan of this music and so I could only assume, from the volume and musical genre and from the placement of the speakers, that this was done to be disruptive of our service. For whatever reason, my righteous indignation got the best of my youthful self and I lost it.

In a huff, I left the church and marched next door. I knocked on the door and told the woman that she was "the most despicable human being I had ever met in my life." Almost a half century has passed since then, and I can still remember exactly what I said. Clearly, this was not a great way to begin a negotiation, nor was it humble, kind, or forgiving. I was probably wrong.

As I think back to that day, I am reminded of the 1976 film *Network*, in which Peter Finch plays Union Broadcasting System's long-time anchor Howard Beale. Lamenting the rush to the bottom line of the network, Beale threatens on-air suicide and then, instead of apologizing for his rant, goes on-air and admonishes his viewers on live TV, "I don't want you to protest. I don't want you to riot. I don't want you to write to your congressman, because I wouldn't know what to tell you to write. I don't know what to do about the depression and the inflation and the Russians and the crime in the street. . . . First, you've got to get mad. . . . Get up right now and go to the window, open it, and stick your head out and yell, "I'm as mad as hell, and I'm not going to take this anymore!!"[3]

And yet, God works. I returned to worship, and I remember that the sermon was particularly powerful that day, though in retrospect its power may have had more to do with my heightened emotional state than any words Rev. Dragt—as good as he was—might have said.

Later that same afternoon, a small group of us visited a local nursing home, guitars in hand, and led some residents in worship. Granted, this was not a very radical act—not a "die in" on Broadway or a one-on-one counseling session with a disabled vet who had just returned from Vietnam, or a trip to desperately poor communities in Appalachia or southern Africa. It was a visit to a nursing home—no danger there, just appreciation from some folks restrained by the bonds of age and limited capacity that someone would take the time to care.

I didn't really believe in instantaneous conversion; and yet, as I left the nursing home and was back in my bedroom with the afternoon sun beginning to set, I was struck by the overwhelming need to devote my life to making the world a better place. The intersection of the angry woman standing in her garage, the powerful sermon in the refashioned barn that served as a sanctuary, and leading worship in a place where I was received with gratitude and enthusiasm, all had an impact on me. I didn't seek to dismiss my lashing out at the woman or the tenderness I felt from those in the nursing home. This convergence of emotions prompted me to hear, for the first time, God's call in my life.

There are countless ways that God calls a person, but I knew I "had to" go to seminary and dedicate the rest of my life to bringing hope and help to others. Unlike my initial response to my uncle's optimistic encouragement about putting on his glasses the first thing in the morning and taking them off the last thing at night, this did not feel like a burden. I did not fully understand even what it meant. How do I devote an ordinary life to extraordinary goals? Where would this commitment lead? Yet, I was overwhelmed with joy and conviction that this was the right thing for me to do; in fact, I could do no other.

> There are countless ways that God calls a person.

Much later I would become familiar with Frederick Beuchner's quote that the place God calls you to is that "intersection" (my word, not his) where your deep gladness and the world's deep hunger meet.[4] As I sat in my room, the sunlight fading through my window, it all felt right, and though I did not yet know Beuchner's definition, intuitively, it fit perfectly. Both the joy and the burden of this lifestyle choice would far outweigh the task of putting on and taking off corrective lenses. So, can God call us in the midst of rather mundane circumstances? The answer, for me, is an emphatic yes—if we are attentive to the call and willing to step out in trust.

As social justice advocates, we must be like Eli, encouraging all to hear the voice that calls us forth into everything we were created to be. And we need to help each other tell the truth even when the truth is hard to hear, as did Dr. King: We heed God's call "that one day every valley will be exalted and every hill and mountain shall be made low . . ."; that, despite deadly viruses like Ebola or Zika and the even more virulent plague of intolerance and fear that emanates through headlines from Paris or Syria or the American campaign trail, "we will be able to hew out of the mountain of despair a stone of hope . . ."; that the scourge of racism and sexism and homophobia that still infests our land will be defeated and "we will be able to transform the jangling discords of our nation into a beautiful symphony of brotherhood

> Where does your deep gladness and the world's deep hunger meet?

. . ."; that the board member will sit with the custodian and the cop will break bread with the gang member, and citizens of every color and culture will come together in constructive dialogue in safe spaces devoid of pretense and hidden political agendas, "and when this happens . . . we will be able to speed up the day when all God's children, black and white, Jew and Gentile, Protestant and Catholic will join hands and sing in the words of the old Negro spiritual, Free at last, free at last. Thank God Almighty, we are free at last."[5]

4 | Commas

Never place a period where God has placed a comma.[1]

—*Gracie Allen*

One of the defining involvements in my life came in the early 2000s while I was serving as director of communication for the one-million-member United Church of Christ. Upon my arrival at the national offices in Cleveland, I was frequently asked about creating an identity campaign for the UCC. I continually delayed answering this question, confident that the answer would emerge and we would discover, organically, a phrase that was right for us. The answer ultimately did appear, thanks to some great cooperation among the creative staff we had assembled to design, develop, and produce communication materials for the denomination.[2]

In the middle of the twentieth century, an old vaudeville act made its way to television—*The Burns and Allen Show.* George Burns and Gracie Allen had performed in the vaudeville circuit and had made the transition to this new medium called television. She was zany; he was infinitely patient. Gracie had a habit of asking questions that at first blush seemed obvious or absurd, but as you thought about them, they carried insights and wisdom that challenged common presuppositions and the superficial self-righteousness of our way of life. And whether one liked or disliked the comedy of Burns and Allen, it was clear that in real life they were very much in love. They ended each show with George's tender signature, "Say goodnight, Gracie."

The story goes that when Gracie died, she left her personal papers for her husband, and with them, a brief note that said, in part, "Never place a period where God has placed a comma. Love, Gracie."

This story about Gracie Allen struck a chord with me. If there was a better phrase to describe the distinctive voice of that "heady and exasperating mix" that I had come to know as the United Church of Christ, I hadn't heard it. So, with due deference to Gracie, we took her admonition and added a graphic element—a large comma—and the phrase "God is still speaking." This became the core of the UCC's multifaceted identity campaign.

In 1959, my predecessor in the UCC, Dr. Everett Parker, formed the Office of Communication of the United Church of Christ, Inc. The Office of Communication was an independent organization within the UCC whose express purpose was to ensure that historically marginalized communities—especially women and people of color—had access to the airwaves. In 1967, based on a suit filed by the UCC, the Federal Appeals Court ruled that WLBT television in Jackson, Mississippi—the strongest station in the mid-south—must forfeit its FCC license because of its failure to serve the African American community in Jackson. WLBT would routinely eliminate news and information about the civil rights struggle that was swirling about them, replacing news feeds with the slate "Sorry, Cable Trouble." In addition, the court established standing on behalf of the public before the FCC. Prior to this, only corporate entities could challenge license renewals, but in UCC v. FCC, this new precedent empowered citizen groups to petition the FCC, and engaging the media became part of the UCC's DNA.

Society would have us believe that if you are not in the media, you do not exist. But, is that true?

In a media saturated culture, "if you are not on TV (or, to fit our current technology—if you are not on social media) you do not exist."[3] Media—in traditional forms and emerging formats—is essential to our understanding of who we are and how we relate to one another. Into the chaotic mix that seemed to swirl around the UCC in those early days of the current century, we thought it imperative to proclaim in the media the call for justice and radical welcome so that, as the prophet Habakkuk says, "a runner may read it" (Hab. 2:2). If the UCC was to establish its identity in the marketplace of ideas, it was essential to engage the media.

And so we took to the airways. We created an innovative commercial featuring bouncers and a velvet rope in front of a church. The bouncers would only let certain types—white, suburban-looking, nuclear families—past the ropes and into the sanctuary that loomed in the background. People who were poorly dressed, young people, gay people, those with disabilities were excluded.

We tried to air the commercial (we willingly paid standard advertising rates) on several networks and cable channels. CBS and NBC refused, using a series of inconsistent and shifting reasons that pretty much boiled down to the fact that our commercial included a gay couple being turned away and since this was shortly after the hotly debated issue of gay marriage in the 2004 presidential election, the commercial was considered too political and too controversial (how far we have come!). Interestingly, the gay couple—never identified—was visible for only about two seconds of the thirty-second commercial. This controversy, though, established the UCC (and, in some ways, our communications office that was behind the UCC's identity campaign) as a beacon for LGBT justice that would later give rise to Believe Out Loud as a core emphasis of our work at Intersections.[4]

The language of Scripture is the language of image and metaphor—a challenge to our imaginations—and so I was always confused by the critics of the commercial who said, "No church has bouncers and a velvet rope, keeping people out." True. But how many camels have you seen pass through the eye of a needle? Yet, Jesus says that it's easier for that to happen than for you and me—because we are all rich by worldly standards—to get into heaven. Pretty harsh words.

The networks' refusal to air the commercial was a tremendous gift to the church. Through a controversy not of our choosing, the UCC was suddenly catapulted into the limelight in ways that we never could have imagined—or paid for. In the days and weeks following the commercial's rejection, two thousand stories were written about the UCC in major periodicals around the country, and even overseas.[5]

And then, in the spring of 2005, James Dobson decided to attack the animated character SpongeBob SquarePants as being a shill for the "gay agenda." The UCC's general minister and president, Rev. John Thomas, offered an unequivocal welcome to the upbeat squishy guy. Publicity again soared. Social media was just in its infancy, but TV, radio, bloggers, the press loved it! And, again, hundreds of people e-mailed to say thank you for bringing a little whimsy into their lives; thank you for being a religious voice interested in joyful inclusion instead of hateful, bigoted exclusion.

The phrase "God is still speaking" and commas of various sizes and shapes became ubiquitous across the UCC, appearing on planning calendars, as a theme for annual gatherings, on buses and billboards, in radio ads, and on T-shirts, tote bags, banners, and coffee mugs. More than a decade later, the phrase and the symbol were still widely used across the denomination.

On the day of Donald Trump's inauguration as the forty-fifth president of the United States, President Barack Obama—a one-time member of Trinity United Church of Christ in Chicago—may have been drawing upon his UCC roots in his very first post-presidency remarks at Andrews Air Force base. There, he told wary and disheartened followers, "This is just a little pit stop. This is not a period. This is a comma in the continuing story of building America."[6]

Fundamentalist churches took to mocking this identity work with signs, ads, and brochures that proclaimed, "Never place a comma where God has placed a period. God has spoken." But members of the UCC wore their commas proudly, believing in an active, relational God still at work in human history.

There are those who said the UCC's "God is still speaking" campaign was shallow, superficial, without theological merit, but I was there, peering through the one-way glass in our focus groups when person after person told how they were wounded, abused, neglected, and dismissed by the church. I was there as e-mail after e-mail rolled into our office saying "Thank you, thank you. I had almost given up hope."

The prophet Isaiah says, "Ho, everyone who is thirsty, come to the waters. . . . Listen . . . that you may live. . . . You shall call nations that you do not know, and nations that do not know you shall run to you. . . ." (Isa. 55:1–5).

These words, to a people in exile—a people who were overwhelmed and defeated and abused and enslaved by foreign powers—charge the Hebrew people to "listen" so that they might live and then to "call" nations they do not know and to accept previously unknown people who run to them. The desperate, dispirited, dispersed people of Israel are enjoined to reach out to other nations, begging an important question for us in a day where the "other" is often excluded through economic inequality, homophobia, or systemic racism: Who is not here yet?

Who is not here yet?

Likewise, in Luke's Gospel (14:15–24), the banquet is set. The table is prepared. The hour has come. But those who were invited—the landowners and religious professionals, the rich and the famous—well, they had other things to do. But the food will rot if it is not eaten soon and God will not be denied. So go into the highways and the byways—a biblical euphemism for "outside of town" where the rubes and hillbillies live—and invite them in. But there is still more room—indicating just how wide God's bounty is! And so the master instructs the servant to go out even beyond the needy (poor, crippled, blind, and lame) in the town, which is an allusion to the inclusion of the Gentiles. Who is not here yet?

It is often easy to see who is here, although sometimes even those who are present are treated as if they are invisible. But who is absent? Who are the people who feel neglected or rejected by the church? Who has been rejected, dismissed, ignored, or overlooked? How can you reach out with a Christlike embrace in worship, in fellowship, in mission, in education? God's abundant banquet awaits. And still there is room. Who is not here yet? Invite them in and let them know that they are welcome.

God's history continues to unfold around us in ways that are both global and very personal. During this period, I realized how having a voice in the marketplace of ideas requires that you step up boldly and proclaim that in this land of democracy—built on the principle that out of the cacophony created by our rich cultural mosaic, there is a sweet harmony—all voices must be heard.

This is often not an easy pathway. Tolkien says, "It does not do you good to leave a live dragon out of your calculations, if you live near him."[7] And the dragons are many in our chaotic world. But out of the chaos of Pentecost, the church was born. And out of the chaos of the universe, God created the heavens and the earth. Six times in the first chapter of Genesis does God see the world and call it good. Six times. The seventh time, God calls it very good. But nowhere does God say it's perfect and nowhere does God say it's finished.

It is up to us to finish this creative work; and this process often involves taking risk, charting a new course, placing one's reputation, one's career, even one's life on the line. When are such risks worth taking?

I have a colleague, Cliff Aerie, who tells the story about the great idea he got when he was a kid. All the other kids were selling lemonade. He and a friend realized that candy was much more enticing. Who could resist? So they pooled their savings, purchased their inventory, built their stand, and then set it up in their favorite spot—deep in the woods. No one came.

In the midst of the controversy over the commercials, the UCC refused to "hide our light under a bushel," but rather proclaimed the good news of the gospel in bold and innovative ways. The thinking: we cannot give a party where no one comes. The stakes are too high. The church has turned people away too often. We need to take our hospitality into the streets. All a commercial like the one we created for the UCC—and several years later, similar events unfolded when we produced a commercial for Intersections' LGBT justice initiative, Believe Out Loud—can be is a discussion starter, a conversation opener. It is up to individuals who care about justice and inclusion to continue the dialogue, to make people feel welcome and to demonstrate their own personal justice commitment until new friends feel so compelled to join in that they cannot stay away.

Another friend, Vicki McGaw, an ordained minister in the United Church of Christ and, at the time, a trainer for the UCC's Stillspeaking campaign, learned about the rapidly deteriorating health of a man in her congregation who was desperately in need of a kidney transplant or would need to go on dialysis to stay alive. Vicki took a test and discovered she was a match for this man and, after prayer and conversation with her husband, Mike, and their kids, believed that God was speaking to her through this situation. She decided to donate her kidney to this man.

A week before the operation, Vicki and I were talking about the training session she was about to do, and the conversation shifted to her upcoming operation. As I spoke in awe of her generosity, Vicki said "It's really only another expression of hospitality." Another expression of hospitality! This was the depth to which so many of us felt called in this effort and why this effort became a singular point in my life's journey. This was the openness with which Jesus Christ challenged me to be faithful, that I would literally give a part of myself to another and see it as an expression of welcome. No, this was no superficial campaign in which we were engaged. Rather, it was a resounding affirmation of the mantra that continues in use throughout UCC congregations today, that "no matter who you are or where you are on life's journey, you are welcome here."

The comma became a core graphic element in the UCC's stillspeaking identity campaign. The comma separates all that has come before from all that is to follow. It is a common mark of punctuation; the simplicity of the graphic element was part of its appeal. The purpose of punctuation is to separate words, give meaning and cohesion to language, and give expression and emphasis in writing. When I spoke about our "stillspeaking" efforts, my standard presentation was often entitled, "Get, the punctuation, right (?)" and I made the point of how by changing the punctuation, you change its meaning.

Add a period and you have a declaratory sentence: Get the punctuation right.

An exclamation point adds urgency: Get the punctuation right! Capitalize all the letters—GET THE PUNCTUATION RIGHT—and the urgency is compounded, especially in an e-mail or text, when it is considered "shouting."

Add a question mark after the word "punctuation" and then add an exclamation point: "Get the punctuation? Right!" and you have a little conversation.

Incorporate dashes before and after the comma: "Get the punctuation—comma—right," and the comma itself is emphasized.

It was interesting that the comma should play such a big part in the identity emphasis of the United Church of Christ. Throughout my career, it had been a professional objective to offer new insights into ancient texts in order to make these age-old lessons fresh and relevant to our complex and rapidly changing world. I'd often say that I taught Bible study "without the commas" and without deference to designations of chapter and verse—which, | Get the punctuation right. | of course, were much later devices, inserted to help us organize our understanding and descriptions of these sacred times. But, upon reflection, I was promoting a hermeneutic not restrained by convention or presupposed paradigms; for such restraints often kept us from experiencing the fullness of God's grace, the opportunities for God's surprise and the implications of God's call.

The title of this narrative points to the punctuation mark that separates all that goes before from all that follows. It is an appropriate demarcation for each of us in that during every instance of our lives, we encounter the eternal moment where past and future meet. Death, then, becomes the ultimate comma—the one aspect of life's journey we all share, complete with its accompanying uncertainty, fear, dread, grief, sense of loss, and—*in sha'Allah* (God willing)—hope for a peace that passes all understanding on the other side of the grave. The expression "beyond the comma" calls us to recognize, realize, even celebrate, those moments that continuously offer the possibility that at these comma-points, qualitatively new opportunities confront us. It is incumbent upon us to act on these comma moments and make the most of the "intersections" that follow.

It is significant, then, that my personal discovery's starting point took place during the time of my role as communications director for an entire denomination that was simultaneously discovering new opportunities for mission and ministry and using the comma as a central element in that process. So, while this narrative is basically about how the commas in one's life lead to intersections, both personal and corporate, if we are to be attentive to both at the neglect of neither, then those comma points are beginning points for how we become more fulfilled individuals.

The first time I recall using the phrase "beyond the comma" was during the funeral service I performed for my father-in-law, Jim Anderson. As I constructed the service, there was an image in my head that I could not shake. In his later years, Jim had a couple of cats. It was his habit to walk down his gravel driveway to get the morning paper, his cats trailing behind, backlit as the dappled sunlight

Death is the ultimate comma.

cast glimmering shadows on the driveway path. The scene was profoundly peaceful, almost heaven-like, and it was in this context that I used the image in my funeral homily: with the fever of life over, with the burden of decision-making completed, Jim was now free, "beyond the comma."

It became an image for me that defined eternal life anew, seared into my consciousness. The visual image was the very embodiment of what the afterlife represented for me. Except for one thing: it was not real. In order to retrieve the morning paper, Jim had to walk east, and so the sun could not have been at his back. Yet, the image lingered—and lingers still—as the unimaginable possibility of moving beyond the comma—the pauses that redirect our lives. And so, for me, this image became the précis for the remainder of my life. The purpose of the comma is to offer a pause between all that has come before and all that will ultimately follow. In a very real sense in my own life, this pause created the experience of, and understanding about, the vital role that intersections can play in deepening the understanding of what it means to be fully alive.

Again we look to the poetic inventiveness of e. e. cummings, perhaps the best ever to capture the possibilities of punctuation as a window into new paradigms and images. His use of spacing, capitalization, verb tenses, spelling, and punctuation challenges the senses as his poems cascade across the page in unusual ways. One poem, "since feeling is first," underscores the power of such imagery, ending with the lines:

for life's not a paragraph
And death I think is no parenthesis[8]

Life is not a paragraph, and death, I think, is no parenthesis. As Oscar Wilde wrote, "We are all in the gutter, but some of us are looking at the stars."[9]

It is not only punctuation, but also emphasis that gives rise to the magnificent mosaic that is our human condition. In any given gathering, if participants were to introduce themselves to an alien life form, it would be hard for the extraterrestrials to tell the difference between those in the room and the population at large. But those who were gathered would know there *are* differences. Individuals are often passionate about the uniqueness of their identity, which is registered in the emphasis we proclaim about ourselves. As we struggle with the truth about who we are and how we engage with others, it is important to be clear about your emphasis.

Back in the sixties I was at a peace rally in Washington, D.C.—actually, it was a counter protest to a pro–Vietnam War, bomb-the-hell-out-of-Hanoi demonstration. One dear soul, an older woman, engaged me on the street trying to tell me how it was my duty as a Christian to bomb the heathen Viet Cong into oblivion. She became increasingly agitated and when she finally realized that she would not be able to convert me to her position, she exploded with fiery venom in her voice: "Well, God bless you!" Her words were gentle; but her tone was brutal and condemning. Be clear about your emphasis. It establishes who you are.

Be clear about your emphasis.

Among my past vocational pursuits was work as a theatre director. A common acting exercise we used to help establish motivation had to do with scooter pies, those chocolate covered desserts with graham cracker inside and a marshmallow center. Some people know them as "s'mores." In the south they call them moon pies. The phrase we used, "I like scooter pies," could be spoken with different emphases to change the motivation. *I* like scooter pies (I don't care if anyone else does). I *like* scooter pies (I don't care what anyone else thinks). I like *scooter* pies (not cherry, not lemon merengue, not strawberry rhubarb—but scooter pies). I like scooter *pies* (ah yes, lip-smacking, scooter pies!).

From miracle cures, to mundane meetings, from the legacy of our ancestors to this morning's sunrise, from headlines that scream out of the daily newspaper to the gentle whisper of affirmation by a trusted friend, from the stirring in your heart when you hear your favorite song to the sound of your grandson when he says "Grandpa, let's go fishing"—be clear about your emphasis and get the punctuation right. There's no doubt that if we but listen, we will know . . . God *is* still speaking.

5 | Faith and Doubt

My coming to faith did not start with a leap but rather a series of staggers from what seemed like one safe place to another.[1]

—*Anne Lamott*

It is not just UCC members or those who feel rejected who have responded to the "God is still speaking" message. One Easter Sunday, I visited a Moravian Church in central Pennsylvania. The pastor concluded his sermon, in the midst of illustrations about Catherine Marshall and Winston Churchill, by saying, "Easter is God's comma, where we would put a period."

Through a controversy not of our choosing, we were given a gift. The question became, "How do we respond to this new reality?" Following up on the Easter illustration, we get some clues from the apostle Thomas in John 20:19–29.[2] Thomas gets a bum rap. For centuries we have branded him with a name that has come to signify stubbornness, superficiality, and weakness of faith. We affix the adjective "doubting" to his name so that Doubting Thomas is said as if it is a single word, doubtingthomas, rendering him one dimensional. Indeed, as I was growing up, I thought of Thomas as barely one rung on the ethical ladder above Judas.

But Paul Tillich reminds us that "doubt is not the opposite of faith, it is one element of faith."[3] And Alfred Lord Tennyson once wrote, "There lives more faith in honest doubt than in half the creeds."[4]

Imagine the scene in Jerusalem during that first Easter. Within the space of a single week, the triumphant entry into Jerusalem went horribly wrong. Judas, one of the inner circle, one of Jesus' closest friends, betrayed him and then killed himself. Peter, another close friend, denied him publicly three times within hours. The crazed crowd demanded his death. He was tortured and crucified between common criminals. He died before he could even be anointed and then when the women went to the tomb after the Sabbath, they reported that someone had stolen the body. Clearly it was not safe.

When a group of disciples gathered behind closed doors, Jesus appeared. Just like that. Thomas, who was not present, offered an intriguing disclaimer, "Unless I see the mark of the nails in his hands, and put my finger in the mark of the nails and my hand in his side, I will not believe." But a week later, when the disciples gathered again, Thomas was there. Jesus again appeared and challenged Thomas to do what he said—put his fingers in the holes in his hands and the wound in his side. But, Thomas did no such thing. Rather, he exclaimed, "My Lord and my God," the first post-resurrection affirmation in John's Gospel of Christ's divinity.

Thomas needed more data. He would not trivialize his belief, he would not give in to easy assumptions. He had only days earlier been let down by the very friends—Judas, the betrayer, Peter the denier—he assumed would be the most staunch defenders of Jesus. Centuries later, Harry Emerson Fosdick would say, "We need to doubt until we are able to doubt our doubts."[5] Thomas needed more evidence. As Paul Simon wryly sings, "Faith is an island in the setting sun, but proof, yes, proof is the bottom line for everyone."[6]

Once confronted with the evidence, Thomas's faith moved to a whole new level, prompting the affirmation that Jesus is God. Thus, Thomas's initial questioning yielded to a confession that challenged the doubts in the rest of us. As Frederick Buechner writes, "Doubt is the ants in the pants of faith. Doubt keeps faith awake and moving."[7]

To quote Harry Emerson Fosdick:

Fear imprisons, faith liberates;

Fear paralyzes, faith empowers;

Fear disheartens, faith encourages;

Fear sickens, faith heals;

Fear makes useless, faith makes serviceable;

Fear puts hopelessness at the heart of life, while faith rejoices in its God.[8]

Organizational development guru Peter Drucker is widely quoted as having said, "People who take risks generally make about two big mistakes a year. People who don't take risks generally make . . . about two big mistakes a year."[9]

If we are to be faithful, we too are called to risk, to go forward boldly and creatively into a world where we will be unable to hide from media exposure, even though we cannot predict our final destination. We must proclaim who we are and offer Jesus' extravagant welcome all along the way. We must engage the society that surrounds us. We must speak truth to power. The time is *now*. The task is *ours*.

One of my favorite columnists has always been Frank Rich, formerly of the *New York Times*. His words are bold and insightful. In early December 2004, I spoke at length with his office about the UCC's ad controversy. A few days later, a friend whom I hadn't heard from for decades called me, all excited because he had received an advance copy of Frank Rich's upcoming column, and he told me I was in it. I was proud! My career was now complete! I was quoted by Frank Rich! So Sunday came, I got my copy of the *Times,* and I started reading quickly—the first paragraph, then the next, the next . . . Then, I saw it—near the end of the article—my name in Frank Rich's

> We are not very
> exciting guests.
> Oh, really?

column. My eyes leapt to the paragraph where my name appeared. The quote seemed painfully brief, but I was confident it would be profound. Just six short words: "We are not very exciting guests." I guess my career wasn't complete after all.

The context of what I said in my interview was that those in the church, who labor day in and day out in the trenches, aren't provocative or argumentative enough to be classified as media stars or celebrities or provocative pundits of faith; and so we are not very exciting. But we *are* engaged with people every day who understand the triumphs and tragedies of real life and whose stories are dynamic and compelling and transforming. These stories represent the moral values that should be considered in the media.

So our first task is to say, "No matter who you are or where you are on life's journey, you are welcome here." In essence—we are saying, "Come!" The invitation includes an exclamation point—for emphasis—not as a command, but as a celebration, so that it is genuinely meant: Come! Next, we are to "Go." Our life's task, then, is to "Come and Go." I still recall that this is the title of the first sermon I ever heard preached by Rev. Gordon Dragt, the person who was to become my minister in my college years and the one most responsible for shifting my life's journey. If we are to be faithful, we too are called to go forward boldly and creatively into our complex world, even though we cannot predict where we will end up.

How do we go? And where do we go? Perhaps we can find a clue in the Scriptures. In Genesis 12:1–4a we read:

> Now the LORD said to Abram, "Go from your country and your kindred and your father's house to the land that I will show you. I will make of you a great nation, and I will bless you, and make your name great, so that you will be a blessing. I will bless those who bless you, and the one who curses you I will curse; and in you all the families of the earth shall be blessed." So Abram went, . . .[10]

God offers a good three-point sermon to
Abram. The first point is the command "to go." Dr.
Ephrain Agosto, formerly of Hartford Theological
Seminary, spoke of an intense study undertaken
around the Hebrew word that has been translated
here. Experts from across the country gathered and offered papers and perspectives. After significant scholarly input and intellectual deliberation, the
conclusion was that the Hebrew word translated as "go" actually means "go."

Come . . . and Go.

Simple. Direct. Don't just sit there. Go.

The second point is that God does not say where to go—"to a place
that I will show you." At the time of departure, there is no land of milk and
honey, but there *is* a "promised land" because God says that God *will* show
Abram where to go . . . just not yet.

The third point is that God offers Abram greatness, a blessing, if he goes.
He will not be able to hide in the shadows but his light will shine on the
hill. The implications for our contemporary call in the world seem obvious.

Because—as Genesis says—Abram went. No hesitation, no elaboration. He just went. And his name became blessed. If we are to be faithful,
we too are called to go forward boldly and creatively into a world where we
will be unable to hide from media exposure, even though we cannot predict
our final destination. So a lesson for life's direction can be summed up in
these two words, "come" and "go." These words began the process that
shifted my whole life. Can they do so for you, as well?

6 | The Other

> You, Dear Reader—You are Amazing Grace.
>
> You are a Precious Jewel. . . .
>
> Only you and I can help the sun rise each coming morning.
>
> If we don't, it may drench itself out in sorrow.
>
> You—special, miraculous, unrepeatable, fragile, fearful, tender, lost,
>
> sparkling ruby emerald jewel, rainbow splendor person. It's up to you.[1]
>
> —Joan Baez

Whether in matters intensely personal or between nations and races, nonconformity can be a positive force, opening a door to new directions, signaling innovative solutions to intractable problems. But at the end of the day, we all want to be part of a group, to belong. We cannot escape the differences between us, and celebrating diversity is an expression of justice and hospitality. This was obvious to me, but my experience at Intersections has indicated that it is not obvious to all. I am always surprised when I am told that our work at Intersections is "courageous," when it seems so logical. We simply provide a framework for people to talk together. How is this courageous? And why did the principle of empathy for "the other" become so important to me personally?

When I was about eleven years old, my parents decided that I should take guitar lessons, giving me a constructive outlet and, they thought, making an investment in my future that would last a lifetime. Their motives in this laudable decision were irrespective of whether or not I wanted to take guitar lessons or had any natural musical ability.

Like most of my Levittown neighbors, we were staunchly middle class, filled with aspirations of a better life for (white) post–World War II veterans' families. Like others, we had only one car. My dad commuted to work on the Long Island Railroad and took our car to the train station every day, where it sat for hours awaiting his return. Except on special days when my mother would need to run errands, we had no access to automobile transportation throughout the day. I had to walk about a mile to my instructor— along one of the busiest thoroughfares in the neighborhood.

I was very tall—close to six feet (remember, I was eleven) and "blessed" with an early and acute case of acne. My height reinforced my near-sightedness, and the glasses I first wore publicly with Phil Sheridan had become very thick. I embodied the term "four eyes." I always wore dress pants because I couldn't get jeans to fit—a detriment that I compensate for even deep into my sixties where my default wardrobe continues to feature successor brands to Wrangler and Levi Strauss.

I carried a large, old classical guitar case—no sleek electric model fashionable in the day—and I still wince at the pain and embarrassment (a fate worse than death for an awkward eleven-year-old) at being laughed at and mocked by teens cruising past in cars or walking the streets in groups I so wanted to be part of. Their comments were biting and cruel as teenage comments can be. Their taunts made me feel forever different—unworthy, embarrassed, unsure of myself, awkward—just different in so many ways.

But I later realized that it was through this repeated experience (every friggin' Tuesday!) that I first began to empathize with the marginalized. The incident was strongly symbolic for me and I have long come to understand the power of symbols in shaping attitudes and actions. As I grew into adulthood, and the stakes became higher, I continued to view reality through the eyes of a gangly, acne-prone, nearsighted kid walking alone with an oversized guitar case down Jerusalem Avenue in Levittown—true, Jerusalem Avenue—and understanding in a visceral way, one I could not yet articulate, how unsettling and isolating it can feel to be "other."

Much later, during seminars and exercises about white privilege, I would use this experience as an illustration of why I had empathy for those who experience intolerance, hostility, and even violence because they are perceived as different. Usually my description would evoke blank stares, condescending looks, or disbelieving nods. I was, after all, a tall, straight, successful white guy. What could I possibly know about being marginalized? How could I possibly understand in the pit of my stomach what it means to be on the receiving end of racist taunts or homophobic stares? It was frequently clear to me that the level of empathy in such settings—usually full of well-meaning liberals—did not extend to awkward eleven-year-olds walking alone amidst catcalls and shouts of derision.

As Pakistanis went to the polls in 2013 seeking their first democratic transition after a full-term civilian-led government, Americans most frequently heard a narrative about Pakistan as a largely violent and lawless nation, steeped in corruption and plagued by extremism. But this is only part of the story in this diverse and strategically important country with a large diaspora in the United States. Into this media narrative, Intersections led its annual multifaith delegations of U.S. religious leaders, community organizers, scholars, and students to meet with Pakistani counterparts.[2] On our repeated visits, we Americans experienced extraordinary Pakistani hospitality; we discovered a remarkable openness—a hunger even—for conversation with religious and community leaders, professors, students, and grassroots activists. We spent a lot of time listening (thank you, Phil

Sheridan and Samuel) and heard a perspective that, though sharply critical of U.S. foreign policy (as well as their own), was equally committed to finding mutuality in combatting social problems in our respective societies.

Our US-Pakistan Interreligious Consortium (UPIC) delegations were continuously met with an eagerness for engagement. We spoke with religious and community leaders, professors, students, and grassroots activists. There was much to learn as we sought to "change the story" in both countries. We knew the American side of the equation: the cost in American lives and limbs and the huge financial investment in the Global War on Terror; the resentment we felt toward Pakistan for being a mercurial ally at best, for harboring Osama bin Laden, for blasphemy laws used to persecute Christians and other religious minorities, and for atrocities against women.

> Spend a lot of time listening.

But what about the Pakistani side? Were we in the United States aware that the Global War on Terror had claimed more than forty thousand Pakistani lives? Could we imagine the terror inflicted on a whole population caused by drone strikes, and then the humiliation we heaped on top of the pain because we refused to officially acknowledge that the strikes occurred? We learned that a shift to human security—beyond military security and towards improving the quality of life in terms of education, health care, and good governance—might prove more effective in achieving better U.S.-Pakistani relations than past diplomatic efforts.

During our visit in 2013, Dr. Mumtaz Ahmad, then director of the Iqbal International Institute for Research and Dialogue at IIU, informed us about surveys indicating that overwhelming majorities of Pakistanis believed the war on terror was actually a war on Islam, that Jews and Christians were in a U.S.-led conspiracy against Muslims, and that Americans were behind the periodic social unrest in Pakistan in order to break apart the country, so that the United States could seize or dismantle the Pakistani nuclear arsenal. Sobering words. The fact that the evidence for this was slim or nonexistent was immaterial to Pakistanis. Facts often have little to do with fears or perceptions, as subsequent rhetoric throughout the 2016 U.S. presidential campaign demonstrated. Remember, too, that at the same time one in six Americans believed President Obama was a Muslim and more than 10 percent of Americans thought Joan of Arc was Noah's wife.[3]

We also spoke with female students from IIU's Critical Thinking Forum. Their approach to problem solving was assertive, inquisitive, and truly inventive and clearly does not fit the narrative we read about Pakistan in the States. I had the distinct impression that we were meeting with the next generation of Pakistani leaders. And that should give us all great hope, especially as we recall that 55 percent of all Pakistanis are under age twenty-five.[4] We discussed how many social issues facing Pakistan also reverberated across the United States. Disparity of income, unemployment, human rights concerns, dysfunctional government, and lack of constructive outlets for young people were issues common to both nations.

While we clearly encountered differences in culture, governance, and economic stability, we wondered if there were things we could learn from each other to help salve social wounds in our respective countries. We wondered if working for social justice was a space where we might find common ground. The answer in our conversations was a resounding yes on both counts. Sitting at the table together marked a clear beginning of meaningful exchange and progress on deepening interpersonal relationships.

One singular challenge was raised time and again: what difference can religious leaders make in a country that is beset with deep and abiding problems like poverty, unemployment, a dysfunctional educational system, extremist violence (isn't religion the problem here?), and profound distrust in the government's ability to right the ship? These are largely Pakistani issues and, as we were told, best left for the Pakistanis to solve. But these are social issues that also reverberate across the United States. Were there things we could learn from each other to help salve these similar social wounds in our respective countries? Dr. Masoom Yasinzai, rector of IIU, addressed our group: "Religious leaders speak from the pulpit of conscience and not from the soapbox of politicians."[5]

When the time came for us to create our action agenda, we sought to have a deep impact, but we also wanted our objectives to be reachable. Three elements came into focus. First, we agreed to continue meeting. Pakistani-American relations have been fraught with fits and starts. In Pakistan, governments come and go, official programs begin and are then abandoned, and the lack of staying power through such transitional times on the part of Americans was deeply resented. Americans are quick to lose patience and abandon programs before they have a time to take root. If our UPIC delegation was to have any long-term impact, our own internal commitment to one another was essential. And so we agreed to meet again and we agreed that we would add a stronger youth contingent from both countries.

A second area of cooperation emerged around exchange programs. Our delegation was composed of not only religious leaders but also representatives from several institutions of higher education.[6] We discussed the reality that opportunities for U.S. students to study in Pakistan were almost non-existent[7] (insurance companies did not want to incur the liability); we were determined to find ways to overcome this obstacle so that more Americans could study there, believing this to be the best way to deepen understanding of Pakistan free from media bias.

The third area concerned the problematic issue of drones. Parts of two days had been devoted to a discussion about U.S. drone strikes (with Pakistani government complicity). I always believed that the most terrifying aspect of drones was that they are silent killers, but I learned that what terrorizes whole communities about drone warfare is that they are *not* silent. In rural villages, the constant hum of drone engines is audible and serves as an ever-present reminder that instant death looms just overhead. Further, in a society built on the principle of modesty, it was widely known that drone cameras could penetrate roofs and walls, leaving Pakistanis feeling vulnerable to the roving eyes of foreign intruders. The psychological toll from this aspect of drone warfare cannot be overstated.

After much discussion, LUMS law professor, Uzair Kayani suggested we begin a joint U.S.-Pakistani campaign to raise money to help rebuild the

lives and communities where drone strikes occur. This was core to what religious groups have always done: help people in need as they reclaim their
lives. At the same time, such an effort would raise the moral questions surrounding drone warfare and increase the profile of U.S. policies and their
failure to acknowledge the damage done—a deep affront to the national
honor of Pakistanis. Further, by implicitly acknowledging the Pakistani government's involvement, such a joint effort by both Americans and Pakistanis
would demonstrate solidarity. Springing from faith-based convictions across
sectarian lines, this would make a powerful, nonpolitical statement. While
this goal was laudable, the practical obstacles proved too great for a fledgling
group like UPIC to overcome, and—as of this writing—this dimension of
our work has yet to be realized in any meaningful way.

We left Pakistan with an actionable agenda that included a commitment to continue meeting, using the educational institutions we represented—Pakistani and American—as starting points for face-to-face
exchanges between our two countries. While the agreement to undertake
a joint effort to rebuild the lives and communities of those affected by
drone strikes proved too ambitious for us, grass roots relationship building
between societies that have recently had such a profound level of suspicion
between them was no small feat. Will these efforts prove fruitful? Ultimately, time will tell. But the eagerness we discovered among Pakistanis
to engage Americans in order to repair a fractured relationship was a deeply
hopeful sign. The late Dr. Mumtaz Ahmad, a vital Pakistani partner in this
venture, wrote to us that these efforts had reduced the suspicion between
our two countries.[8]

One of the young people we met, Shanzae Asif, an undergraduate Pakistani student, later came to New York as a summer intern for Intersections.
While here, Shanzae had a chance meeting with Elizabeth Dabney Hochman,
executive director of KidSpirit, a nonprofit online magazine and community
by and for youth to engage each other about life's big questions in an open
spirit. Its mission is to promote mutual understanding among 11- to 17-year-
olds of diverse backgrounds and support their development into world citizens

with strong inner grounding. At the time, KidSpirit had satellite editorial boards across the United States and in India, but nothing in Pakistan.

Inspired, Shanzae offered to establish such a board among students at her former school in Karachi. Years later, this board, along with a new one in Lahore, has grown and is thriving. KidSpirit representatives made a presentation about their work and our partnership during a subsequent UPIC visit. One Pakistani student, seventeen-year-old Ammara Mohsin, wrote an essay "Rising Above Borders" about the intractable dispute between India and Pakistan. Her essay was published by KidSpirit in its fall 2014 magazine issue, *Discovery and Progress*, and also in the Huffington Post in honor of World Peace Day in 2014. She asks a key question, "Are the borders that divide us more important than the thousand reasons that unite us?"[9] The article captured the true spirit of our UPIC work and debunked the pessimism of those who profess there are irreconcilable differences between us. Her message is so powerful, it merits repeating:

It was with much excitement over the prospect of being able to visit a different country, albeit from afar, that I visited the Indo-Pak Wagah Border in Lahore.

This is the boundary dividing India and Pakistan, with the eastern half of the Wagah village in India and the western half in Pakistan. I am from Pakistan, and as our car came to a screeching halt some miles away from the border gate, so did my anticipation. A whirlwind of emotions hit me. The first was disappointment, for India and Pakistan are as similar as a pair of monozygotic twins. Where was the "other country" I was promised?

Secondly, I felt profound confusion. I couldn't fathom why the rivalry between these two countries existed when they are so similar. Then disappointment came swirling around again, this time coupled with anger about the loss that both of these nations in particular, and humanity in general, incur by twisting a potential friendship into such pronounced enmity.

The border looked as though a mirror had been placed in the middle of the gates. The scene was painted in green, red, orange, and white; the colors of both nations' flags. The two flags stood together at the entrance gates, tall and proud. Border guards with stern expressions stood as erect as buildings. A huge crowd had gathered, and they watched in awe as the magnitude of the situation slowly dawned on them.

Patriotic songs of both countries were played and were accompanied by loud chants of *Pakistan zindabad* ("Long live Pakistan") and *Bharat mata ki jai ho* ("Victory for Mother India"). Sitting on a balcony step, watching the synchronized parade of soldiers from each country, I couldn't help but smile. I smiled because I saw there was nothing here to hate. These are just people like us sitting across an imaginary line. I smiled because there is so much that unites us.

This perceived wall does not only exist between India and Pakistan, it occurs within countries all across the globe. We have, for some reason, decided to attribute more importance to nationality, geography, or religion, instead of focusing on our similarities: our sense of self, values, and ethics.

There are many reasons to care about people across different country's borders, be it food, festivals, cultural heritage, even hospitality. We can have the best things that each country has to offer if we only embrace each other with open arms and warm hearts. All we need to do is ask ourselves: are the borders that divide us more important than the thousand reasons that unite us? After all, we are all human beings and are taught the same basic principles.

As I scrutinized the solemn expressions on the faces of the people present, I could see that many of them had undergone this epiphany. I couldn't help but feel our overwhelming similarities, not just those of race, values, or culture, but our common humanity and shared capacity to love. Once this is understood, the borders blur and become mere dividers of geography, not affecting our sense of self, and certainly not dictating how we behave with our fellow human beings.

In this moment, I realized that there is hope. Not all has to be lost to hatred or the lust for power. We can progress, we can rise above the lines that separate. We can explore the capacity for love, sharing, and tolerance.[10]

While UPIC's ultimate goal was to impact policy makers, who would have thought that, in a few short years, we would have had such a direct impact on Pakistani teenagers? Yet, it is exactly in the unknown, open-ended quality of sharing thoughts and feelings in a safe space that we can uncover the most profound examples of personal transformation. The threads of change weave together into brilliant and unexpected tapestries. This is why I am no longer surprised by the unexpected results of this work.

Several years ago, I had the privilege of interviewing Lutheran theologian and dean of Harvard Divinity School Krister Stendahl. I vividly recall his profound wisdom, punctuated with his distinctive

> Are the borders that divide us more important than the thousand reasons that unite us?

Swedish accent, as he spoke about the importance in the book of Hebrews, "Be not forgetful to entertain strangers, for thereby some have entertained angels unawares" (Heb. 13:2 KJV).[11] Could that have been a twinkle in his eye that I detected as he spoke? Whatever may be the case, his profound love and respect for the sacred text could not be denied. Despite my liberal leanings, there are some terms from the King James Version of scriptures that subsequent translations just cannot capture, and his enthusiasm for this passage sparked my own imagination in ways I did not yet comprehend.

7 | Sacrifice

Come away, O human child!
To the waters and the wild
With a faery, hand in hand,
For the world's more full of weeping than you can understand.[1]

—W. B. Yeats

" I t was the best of times, it was the worst of times, it was the age of wisdom, it was the age of foolishness, it was the epoch of belief, it was the epoch of incredulity, it was the season of Light, it was the season of Darkness, it was the spring of hope, it was the winter of despair, we had everything before us, we had nothing before us, we were all going direct to Heaven, we were all going direct the other way—in short"[2] . . . times much like today.

I remember reading these opening words from Dickens' A *Tale of Two Cities* for the first time like it was yesterday. His novel is set during the

French Revolution when the world seemed rent asunder between the egalitarianism and freedom that the revolution promised, and the very excesses of the revolution itself, as those who stood for the rights of the common citizen became intoxicated with their own power.

The main character—Sydney Carton—is a brilliant but flawed lawyer, filled with self-loathing. He defends Charles Darnay—his alter ego, with whom he has an uncanny physical resemblance. Darnay is successful in love and life. Carton is in love with Darnay's wife Lucy, even though he knows that he can never experience life with her.

Darnay is wrongly accused in the sweep of revolutionary fervor and faces execution at the hands of Madame DeFarge. After converting to Christianity, Carton literally swaps places with him and is marched off to the guillotine in his stead.

His closing thoughts, as an innocent man on the way to the gallows, are among the most poignant lines in all of English literature: "It is a far, far better thing that I do than I have ever done. It is a far, far better rest that I go to, than I have ever known."[3]

This story had a powerful impact on me as a young boy, probably because as a thirteen-year-old I, too, was filled with my share of self-loathing, wondering how someone so insignificant could make a real contribution in a world that even then seemed to be getting increasingly complex and out of control. I saw Sydney Carton as a hero and wondered, since he made his sacrifice in anonymity, if God might truly reward him with that "far, far better place." For, surely, no one else would. Self-loathing is not a helpful emotion, but understanding one's limitations is an important first step in realistically identifying how to structure your life.

Reading A Tale of Two Cities also triggered a sense of justice and sacrifice that would become cornerstones of the value system that would guide my adult life, lead me to seminary, and then focus my ministry on the things that make for peace and human dignity. And reading this literary classic did one other thing: it taught me about irony and paradox: tenets, I would much later come to learn, that are central to the Christian faith—how the king of peace was born in a stable, how the Christ is both human and divine, how the last shall be first, how you must die to live—and how we are called to hold these conflicting realities in tension in order to live lives worthy of our faith.

It has taken a lifetime to navigate the strands of this irony so that I can sort out how my life matters. Unlike Carton or Jean Valjean, the principle character in *Les Miserables*, I have not yet had the opportunity to stand in for a saintly man wrongly accused. In a pivotal scene in *Les Miserables*, the lead character Jean Valjean is confronted with the knowledge of mistaken identity as someone is arrested in his stead, prompting him to decide if he should reveal his true identity. The poignant libretto articulates his dilemma:

He thought that man was me
Without a second glance
That stranger he has found
This man could be my chance![4]

Valjean concludes that because he has made a bargain with God to always be righteous, if he does not confess to who he really is, he would be eternally condemned, and so he confesses, thereby sending his life into an ever-consuming spiral from which—in the show's final scene—he is restored to spiritual wholeness as he is reunited with his daughter, Cosette. For me, the power and the poignancy of *Les Miserables* has had as great an impact on my life as any sacred text. This central symbolic marker in my life was made all the more potent when, a generation ago, I saw the Broadway show with my daughter Kierra, who was studying Victor Hugo's novel in high school, and then twenty-five years later, as I repeated the Broadway experience with *her* daughter, Sonoma, who was only nine at the time.

I don't know if I would have the courage if such a possibility arose. I know only that I continue to struggle with self-worth, comparing my life to those I encounter in real time or in the media whose lives seem more forgiving, heroic, self-sacrificing, helpful than my own. In this very personal wrestling—certainly not unique to me—is there a more universal truth about who we are and what we believe about ourselves?

So I ask explicitly, as a surrogate for those who also wonder about their purpose in life: Is there something in the intersection of past and present, macro and micro, personal and universal that can offer clues about our value as individuals? When my daughter Kristin was in the second grade, she had this marvelous little book, entitled *IALAC*.[5] It was about a little child who woke up in the morning with a sign saying, "I Am Lovable and Capable" (IALAC) around her neck and, as she went through her day, parents, teachers and friends continued to tear little pieces off the sign, symbolic of how we encounter individuals throughout our days who, through their insensitivity, apathy, or neglect slowly destroy our self-esteem, rendering us ever less powerful, less creative, less helpful in our ability to reach out to others.

A generation later, my six-year-old granddaughter Sonoma was participating in a church pageant on the Sunday before Easter. She was a member of the crowd, and the pageant took the children of the congregation on a journey through the events of Holy Week, moving through the Hosannas of Palm Sunday to shouting for release of Barabbas and the condemnation of Jesus just five days later. Two themes that we touched on, with the use of simple choreography, were betrayal and forgiveness. After reading about how Judas betrayed Jesus, I asked both the church school and the congregation to turn their backs on the cross at the front of the sanctuary. I stood down the aisle towards the back of the room and I asked whether anyone had betrayed—or gone against—something their parents or teachers or Jesus had said even though they knew it was wrong.

> I Am Lovable and Capable.

Sonoma, who was really into character as a member of the Jerusalem crowd, was sitting on the rug in the aisle. She looked every bit the part of a Middle Eastern child as her dark, wide eyes were like deep pools beneath the scarf that covered her head. She looked straight at me, eyes filled with imagination, as she shook her head and silently whispered, "nooo."

My heart melted in response to this expression of innocence. Of course my next line was that we all do this, contradicting the complete surrender she had made to her position that she would never do such a thing. I am sure she has no memory of this contradiction, but I wondered how that moment might have been just one of those many things that happen in our lives when we grow from innocence to experience, when the symbolic IALAC card around her neck was ripped just a bit more. It made me profoundly sad.

So, what do we do with this? How do we live with the loss of innocence, of confidence, of self-esteem? A starting point might be found in a wise comment I heard from Fr. Al Burke, a chaplain at Holy Name Hospital in Teaneck, New Jersey, when I was serving as pastor there. We were in a small Bible study group that gathered weekly over a period of years, as clergy supported one another through the triumphs and tragedies of life—unruly parishioners, staff changes, divorces, the death of a spouse. And when those moments of doubt and despair seemed overwhelming, Al would remind us of his definition of faith: belief in God's goodness despite all apparent evidence to the contrary.

In the loss of innocence, in the movement from the garden to the city, from darkness to light, in the recurring cyclical nature of life, we can—if we are attentive—experience birth in the midst of death, hope in the midst of fear, experience that leads to growth and change and new possibilities even in the loss of innocence. This, too, is part of Dr. King's interrelated structure of reality and, if we are attentive and thankful, we can celebrate the movement from innocence to experience, from youth to maturity.

> Faith is belief in God's goodness despite all evidence to the contrary.

The celebration of Passover is when families gather, Seders are shared, matzos broken, prayers sung, and a history recited and remembered. On the eve of Passover in 2014, events would signal a special lesson—not new, really, but given renewed emphasis—beyond the biblical narrative, challenging Jews and Gentiles alike to take stock in the true meaning of the season of remembrance about how we are called in our day to relate to one another across lines of difference.

On this night a madman erupted in a violent tirade outside the Jewish Community Center of Greater Kansas City and nearby Village Shalom, a senior living facility, killing three people.[6] The perpetrator spewed anti-Semitic slurs as he was arrested, exemplifying the rootedness and power of mindless bigotry. The incredible irony that none of his victims were Jewish only deepened the senselessness of an already senseless act, disproving the theory of those who claim to tell the differences between us, even when physical attributes mask them. So blinded by prejudice was the killer that he did not realize his victims were non-Jews.

As tragic as this incident was, it was only a glimpse of things to come. By Passover's end, we learned about leaflets distributed in the Ukraine demanding that Jewish students "register" or risk being deported.[7] While there was much dispute about who was responsible for these leaflets, that is really beside the point. The fact that in the twenty-first century Jewish people can awaken to news of registration and deportation based on religion or ethnicity is beyond terrifying. It is one thing to encounter news about a single maniac at work in the streets of Kansas City; it is quite another to read about leaflets being distributed in an organized way that evokes nightmares of a time when millions of innocent Jews were displaced, dispossessed, and killed.

These two incidents, occurring as horrific brackets around Passover, are familiar reminders that we live in a world where all are *not* free to explore their faith, express their culture, and engage in relationships across lines of difference. The fact that it is Jews who once again were at the focal point of this macabre reality is both baffling and deeply troubling. Like the stain of racism that simply refuses to die, anti-Semitism holds a tenacious stranglehold on the human soul and psyche from generation to generation.

Poignant, sad, grotesque, overwhelming, contemptible—yes, all of these, but none of this should dissuade those of us who care passionately about the human condition from staying the course. We know that the arc of history is long, but we also know that it bends relentlessly towards justice. *We* are the instruments of this justice and it is up to us to ensure our common humanity is celebrated and our inclusive invitation to God's grace is extended to all.

8 | Risk

Live as if you were to die tomorrow.
Learn as if you were to live forever.[1]

—*Mahatma Gandhi*

M any have asked two questions about the work I have done for most of a decade at Intersections: Is it important? And is it effective?

Is it important? I was sharing with a colleague some of the frightening statistics about suicide rates among veterans. Studies show that as many as three times the number of Vietnam vets have committed suicide as were killed in combat, and that now there are also more Iraq and Afghanistan vets who have killed themselves as have died in those conflicts, including the war in Afghanistan—the longest in our nation's history. "Oh, no," my colleague said, "I can't believe those statistics. They can't be right." I shrugged and told him that is what I had heard.

A week later, I saw my colleague again—Mitchell is his name—and he approached me with a trembling voice. "I spoke to my buddy about those statistics," Mitchell said. "I've known this friend for ten years. He's a Vietnam vet although we've never spoken about his service (this, of course, is part of the problem; combat vets are reluctant to speak about the horrors of war with nonveterans). When I shared what you told me, he started to cry. He said, 'I went to Vietnam with a platoon of fifty. Twenty were killed in combat. Twenty-nine have committed suicide. I am the only one left.'"

Does it work? Shortly thereafter, we held a Veteran-Civilian Dialogue at Intersections—one of our programmatic emphases that enables veterans and civilians to gather in a safe space and on a level playing field to share their respective stories about their hopes and fears, traumas and triumphs. Over the years, we've had almost a hundred of these dialogues, involving thousands of participants, veterans and civilians. At the time, we were located on Fifth Avenue, next door to Marble Collegiate Church. Marble had an ongoing and very visible symbol in the city since the beginning of the war in Iraq where, each week, ribbons were placed on the cast iron fence that surrounds the church, and name tags were affixed to the ribbons, representing American service personnel who died in combat in Iraq and Afghanistan.

One of the techniques we used in these facilitated dialogues was to put chairs in the center of a circle and invite participants to sit in those seats and assume the role of soldier or spouse, parent or child, enemy or victim of war and then to interact with one another. Amazing stories—mostly deeply personal—emerged out of this exercise. One person came into the circle and told the story about how he enlisted after 9/11 because he wanted his niece and nephew to continue to experience the freedoms and opportunities that he had grown up with. "I went to Iraq," he said, his voice quivering with emotion, "but a different person came back. I was on edge, addicted to drugs, unpredictable. My niece and nephew were not allowed to be with me."

Then, in the midst of this poignant story, he stopped. The silence in the room was deafening. And after a pause, he said simply, haltingly, with his eyes cast to the floor, "I just saw my buddy's name on the ribbons next door." The poignancy of these few words and the power of the emotion in his voice spoke volumes to veteran and civilian alike about the impact of war on us all.

Another clue to answering the question "where is God's grace in such moments" or, more pointedly, "where is God when *I feel* most alone" is found in the Book of Job. There, we discover the terrible suffering of its principle character.[2] Job asks his friends to stand in solidarity with him in what he believes to be his innocence. But no one does. They rebuke him for his faith and his God for his arbitrary cruelty. This passage reminds us that hospitality does not end with a hug or a handshake or a "have a nice day" or "thank you for your service." Rather, it is integral to a lifestyle that says: I empathize with you, I will share my life with you because we are kin—children of the living God. And by being there for each other, we can be God's presence in one another's lives—even in those moments when we feel most alone. And that is how you know God's love is real.

But let's be honest. Are there not times when each of us feels alienated, isolated, or alone like one of those the bouncers turned away in the UCC's TV commercial or the child whose IALAC sign is chewed into an unrecognizable state? So maybe the question on your mind is: How do *I* know God's love is real? How can it be that God is speaking to *me*? How can this be true? I can barely get my husband to speak to me. My kids don't pay attention. My grandchildren never come see me. My boss barely acknowledges me. My friends never have the time for me. How can you say that God—omnipotent, omnipresent, creator of the universe, very God of very God—is speaking to me?

In the ninth chapter of Luke's Gospel, Jesus and the disciples descend from the Mount of Transfiguration into the valley below.[3] They encounter a crowd and a man whose son is demon-possessed and who calls out to Jesus, "I beg you to look at my son; he is my only child." The Rev. Kate Matthews, retired dean of the UCC's Amistad Chapel in Cleveland and my friend and colleague, states that in his healing of the child Jesus demonstrates what the mountaintop experience means.

God's voice was heard during the glorious episode up on the mountain, but God's power is most dramatically revealed in what happens below, where people are suffering. And it's true, then, that in our own lives, thousands of years later, our experience of God, is inextricably linked to our response to the suffering of the world, and that makes us vulnerable ourselves. Paradoxically, mysteriously, it seems that the closer we draw to God, the closer we draw to one another and to one another's pain.[4] We are all instruments of that power, even if we do not recognize it.

But there's even more. This mirror image cannot be by accident. On the mountaintop, God says, "This is my child, my chosen . . . " and then in the valley, the father cries out, "he is my only child" (Matt. 3:17, Luke 9:38). Can we not see the relationship between the anguish in the man's voice and the poignancy in the words from the cloud about God's child, Jesus, resolutely moving towards Jerusalem and his impending death? Theologian Kimberly Miller van Driel makes an important connection between the voice of God in the cloud and the emotion of a father in the crowd: "This voice was heard at Jesus' baptism, and it resonates again in the desperate plea of the father in verse 38, 'Teacher, I beg you to look at my son, he is my only child.'"[5]

I was speaking as the Christian representative in an annual "Trialogue" at Marble Collegiate Church. Created by the late Arthur Caliandro in the wake of 9/11, an imam, a rabbi, and a minister preach on a Sunday morning from the Marble pulpit and address a specific issue out of their respective faith traditions. In the wake of Hurricane Sandy and the shootings in Newtown, Connecticut, we agreed to focus on the topic of inexplicable tragedy. What do our faith traditions say that can bring a message of healing in such moments?

Uncomfortable as I had been about some of the religious language that emerged out of the shootings at Sandy Hook Elementary School that follow the line of "God's little angels," I offered this instead: We have no rational answer to such things, and to try to fabricate a reason is almost obscenely arrogant and brings no comfort to grieving families. Instead, in the Christian narrative, God's own child, God's chosen, through no fault of his own, suffered humiliation, torture, and a painful death, and so God (the parent) understands—understands our deepest pain. It is not rational, it cannot be answered by Peter's words or building silly dwellings, it is to be experienced—on the mountaintop *and* in the valley.

I experienced this personally in the first week of my tenure as senior pastor of the Presbyterian Church in Teaneck, New Jersey. Five days after I arrived, there was a multiple murder in the community: four children, ages five to eighteen, and their mother were all brutally murdered—shot to death in their home. Wesley Diggs, the father, who owned a tavern in Harellm, was not home at the time and was the family's sole survivor. His family attended the Presbyterian Church—although they were not members—and I ended up doing the funerals.

From the moment I met him, I was convinced of his innocence. I later wrote a book with him about the way he had been immediately labeled as guilty by the police, the news media, and even his friends and colleagues. We became good friends. To this day, the crime has not been solved and he was never charged.[6] The first time I met him, I told him, "I have no explanation. There is no reason why this should have happened to your family." He later told me that my refusal to offer a clichéd answer to his grief was very important to him—actually, the first step in his healing.

> Sometimes, it is okay to say, "I have no explanation."

In the Hebrew Scripture, we discover Jonah—the reluctant prophet—who appears almost as a cartoon character. God's initial call to Jonah is to go east to Nineveh—capital of the Assyrian empire that had many times conquered and oppressed the people of Israel and Judah. Instead, Jonah hops a boat to go west to Tarshish in Spain, the farthest reaches of the known world of the biblical writer. In a great storm, Jonah is thrown overboard but rescued by God when a big fish swallows him whole and spews him back on land (Jon. 1:1–2:10). "There," God again says, "Now, go to Nineveh." So much for running away from the call of God!

Another biblical fish can be found in the first chapter of Mark's Gospel. Jesus encounters Peter and Andrew, then James and John on the shores of the Sea of Galilee. In this exchange, the two sets of brothers respond in a way that is polar opposite to Jonah. They were going about their lives, toiling in the family fishing business. Jesus proclaims, "The time is fulfilled and the realm of God is near. Follow me." And immediately, they put down their nets and follow him. There is no hesitation, no trying to run from God's call. Seven times the Gospel writer uses the word *eutheous*, the Greek word for immediately, to demonstrate the urgency of the call.

But the hopeful message in Jonah is that, despite our trepidation, rationalization, and procrastination, God will not let us go. If it takes a big fish to swallow us whole, that's what God will provide because we are instruments of God's grace—chosen, called, and claimed by God to speak truth to power, to proclaim liberty to the oppressed, to be the word of grace. And it is curious that throughout the story, the cantankerous prophet Jonah leaves behind repentant and worshiping foreigners who, despite his actions, perceive the presence of God in the world and believe in God's redeeming grace (Jon. 3:5–10).

Jonah's stumbling block is that he cannot accept the magnanimity of God's extravagant welcome. He cannot accept that God can be forgiving toward the Ninevites. The story of Jonah is a satire of a kind of discipleship that is neither open nor really understanding of the nature and breadth of God's grace, extended to all humankind.

For us, the point is that even if we are not willing risk-takers like those beside the Galilean lake, but reluctant disciples like Jonah, God will send a big fish—or a tweet—to remind us to go east, not west—so that the open arms of God might be revealed. A question for each of us is what form does the big fish take in our lives? From nagging conscience to personal tragedy to empathy with the suffering of others—how does the often discordant intersection in our hearts and minds, experience and observations challenge our sensibilities and prompt us to act? Attentiveness to our avoidance mechanisms can reduce the anxiety in us and prompt us to boldness and risk-taking that enables us to change the world. And it is, remember, not *our* world. We are but stewards, caretakers of God's created order.

The Creator God is the householder; we are but the managers of creation. All we own is actually God's, entrusted to us for a short time. How we demonstrate our faithfulness is found in our stewardship. Any discussion about faithful stewardship begins with an affirmation of God's sovereignty, an acknowledgement that, as we read God's words in Exodus just before God gives Moses the Ten Commandments, "The whole earth is mine" (Exod. 19:5). Therefore, anything we have, anything we do, anything we are comes from God. And what God has given us is extraordinary.

God will send a big fish.

Allow yourself to be swallowed.

There are many places in Scripture that indicate how we should give; the twenty-fifth chapter of Matthew is but one of them.[7] One of the important elements in this text lies in its position in Matthew's Gospel: it is the final discourse before Jesus' betrayal. So the implication is for us to listen particularly hard at what God is saying to us in these words. Consider also the parable of the talents: A property owner is going on a journey and he gives five talents to one servant, two talents to a second servant, and one talent to a third, then he goes away. No instruction, he just leaves.

This is no big deal to us because we don't have a sense of what it actually means. "Talents" is not meant to imply "skills or traits or abilities" as it does in contemporary English, which has led to untold misdirected sermons in churches around the English speaking world—I've probably been guilty of a score of them myself. Rather, "talents" (Greek *talanton*) in New Testament times is a sum of money—a huge sum of money, which is why the term is used so infrequently in the Bible—only sixteen times, fourteen in this passage. There is no precise way to tell how much money this is, but each talent probably represents three to ten years' income for the common laborer.

So, when we look at the amount that is handed over to the servants, it is a substantial sum. In today's times, if you have a yearly income of $30,000, five talents represents somewhere between $450,000 and $1.5 million dollars, or more! Even the one who received one talent—the person we feel was an afterthought—received between $90,000 and $300,000. Nowhere does the parable say what they were to do with the money; the property owner simply departs without any recorded instruction. But the servants must have known.[8]

Sure enough, when the property owner returns and settles up accounts, the one who received the five talents and the one who received the two talents were greeted with the response: "well done, good and trustworthy slave; you have been trustworthy in a few things, I will put you in charge of many things; enter into the joy of your master. (vss. 21, 22). Here, according to writer and Anglican theologian Chris Haslam, the meaning of the Greek word includes "believing and risk-taking."[9]

But the third servant was afraid and went and buried his talent in the ground. His reward? He was cast into the outer darkness. Why? Answers to this question are not limited to thoughts by contemporary theologians. John Wesley, the founder of Methodism, asks and then answers this question: "Cast ye the unprofitable servant into the outer darkness—For what? What had he done? It is true he had not done good. But neither is he charged with doing any harm. Why, for this reason, for barely doing no harm, he is consigned to outer darkness? He is pronounced wicked, because he was slothful, an unprofitable servant. So mere harmlessness, on which many build their hope of salvation, was the cause of his damnation!"[10]

According to theologian William Loader,

The parable challenges us not to sit on the life of God in us. . . .

If the modern use of talents has any relation to the text, it is at the level of allowing God's life to do its adventures with us and putting our talents (our natural abilities) at God's disposal. The talents of the parable are really about God's life and power, not about our natural abilities. . . .

The tragedy is that many people are afraid of losing or endangering God and so seek to protect God from adventures, to resist attempts at radical inclusion that might, they fear, compromise God's purity and holiness. *Protecting God is a variant of not trusting God.* [italics mine] Matthew wants his hearers to share God's adventure of inclusiveness. God is bigger than our religious industry. . . . We need to encourage people to stop putting God under the mattress.[11]

If we are to be faithful, we are called to risk, to go forward boldly and creatively into a world that seems chaotic. We must proclaim who we are and offer Jesus' extravagant welcome all along the way. We must engage the society that surrounds us. We must speak truth to power. The time is *now*. The task is *ours*.

9 | Art and Culture

There are painters who transform the sun
into a yellow spot, but there are others who . . .
transform a yellow spot into a sun.[1]

—Pablo Picasso

Since Watergate, when political solutions seemed forever tainted, I have looked to the arts as a vehicle for change. In March of 2003, as the invasion of Iraq loomed on the horizon, I confronted the question again as to the role that the arts could play in our consciousness and action. With the horrors of war so close at hand, what right do we have to be celebrating the arts? The world's brokenness was, at that moment, so overwhelming that we could (should?) ask: are we not compelled to expend all our energies, all our skills, all our resources on practical tasks of healing, peacemaking, reconciliation? Shouldn't we be rolling bandages, or giving blood, or collecting food, or writing Congress, or offering ourselves as human shields? I was at a protest rally in Cleveland's Public Square and someone had a sign that read: WWJB? "Who would Jesus bomb?" Shouldn't we at least be carrying signs or doing everything in our power to stop this madness?

In a way, this question focused on the very essence of what it means to be human. Told in Genesis that we've been created in the image and likeness of God—the Creator—means, in part, that we have been given both the ability and the desire to make things. We've been endowed with imagination, and so, as Madeleine L'Engle puts it, we have both the privilege *and* the responsibility to be co-creators with God.[2]

Therefore, the artistic quest is akin to the spiritual quest. It connects the head with the heart and, therefore, it is *essential* to the well-being of our souls. The language of Scripture is the language of image and metaphor, the same as the language of the artist. The artist, like the believer, experiences a strong sense of calling, a calling to bear witness.

Canadian writer and philosopher Sarah Klassen says that in order to best give expression of what is going on—in the world, on the street, in the mind—the artist/witness relies on images. Any reading of the Scriptures reminds us of the power of images: fire, water, the journey, bread, the cross. Images can infiltrate our thinking and change us, for better or worse. Making art is a subversive activity.[3]

> The artistic quest is akin to the spiritual quest.

On a trip to Israel and Palestine, one stop was an elementary school for Palestinian children. Like elementary schools in the United States, kids' artwork adorned classroom walls. Like kids' artwork in the United States, there were bright colors, renderings of families, pets, houses, trees, sunshine. Unlike kids in the United States, there were also scenes of tanks and machine guns, guided missiles and the dead and the dying. It was the way the kids coped with their reality of curfews and blockades and raids by heavily armed Israeli forces in their neighborhoods.

It was sad for me, but this artwork served as an expression of defiance and hope for the kids. It was their way of speaking truth to power, of asserting their humanity, of being co-creators with God against the powers of death and dehumanization that so infiltrated their lives.

The subversive nature of their art did not become fully apparent to me until I was leaving Israel. At the airport in Tel Aviv, since I had videotapes with me, I was exposed to rigorous questions and search by Israeli customs. But when they found a small book filled with some of this children's art and written in Arabic, the probing questions immediately intensified.

Art: hope for the children; subversive to the Israeli government.

And so this is why we have the nerve to celebrate art while the world hovers on the brink of war: because we are creatures caught between terror and amazement.

In *Toward a Christian Poetics*, theologian Michael Edwards says, "The need for stories comes with the exile from Eden. The artist is poised between two worlds, the fallen and the possible."[4] And sociologist Robert Wuthnow reminds us in *Creative Spirituality* that "one of the important contributions of artists in any period is creating narratives and images of wholeness in the face of undeniable brokenness."[5] And there can be little doubt that brokenness abounds in our world.

We are called by God to be among a people who are so hopelessly broken, so alienated from the God of love and peace and mercy and grace that we would even allow ourselves to slip into war; yet we are also a people of possibility, capable of more goodness and beauty and kindness than we could ever ask for or imagine.

In that reality, we are called to be subversive—to speak truth to power—*and* to offer hope, the promise of God's enduring grace. Be clear about your emphasis. Get the punctuation right. It establishes your identity and proclaims who you are.

Biological anthropologist W. C. McGrew finds clues for the definition of culture in the study of primates. McGrew suggests that culture is a process whereby a new pattern of behavior is invented, the innovator transmits this pattern to another, and the one who acquires the pattern retains the ability to perform it long after having acquired it. The pattern spreads across social groups and then endures throughout generations.[6]

While this helps us gain an intellectual understanding of how culture comes about, it says nothing about how important culture resonates in the course of human history or in the hearts of individuals. Our cultural heritage is a connector between us, is based in generational memory and a sense of belonging, and becomes a primary marker of our identities.

But when parts of our identity calcify and consume us, we risk isolation, separating ourselves from those of different cultures, identifying them as "other." Psychological studies show that the fear of one's culture dying is a more powerful threat than the fear of losing one's own life.

Create intersections, not boundaries.

Today, culture can be amplified—but also distorted and eclipsed—by media. Images of all Muslims as terrorists or all Christians as racist cowboys who burn holy texts are distortions that are not only inaccurate but that can lead to social instability and violence. What are principles we should consider in developing a new inclusive paradigm, even a new expansive ethic, for these turbulent times?

First: Create intersections, not boundaries. Intersections prompt new beginnings; boundaries leave us locked in identities and give us an excuse to mistrust and abuse the "other."

Second: Listen. Open the possibility for intersections across culture, socioeconomic groups, races, ethnicities, religious faith and practice. Such interfaith and intercultural dialogues are essential for social healing, and not just among global leaders, but in local communities as well. In conflicted situations, disparate parties are not fully healed until they have an

Listen.

opportunity to tell their own personal stories through their lens of cultural, religious, and ethnic identity. If we seek the things that make for peace, then each of us must take the time to *listen* to the stories of those with whom we differ.

Third: Acknowledge the power of new technology, recognizing that social media has—or shortly will—impact every cultural and religious group on

> Acknowledge the power of new technology and include it in your strategy.

the planet. Community, religious, and ethical leaders must not shrink from it, belittle it, or condemn it. Rather, we need to understand it, especially through the eyes of young people for whom this is a natural way of communicating. Any strategy for global peace must include a media component. We must explore ways to use new technology to enhance the human condition and we must promote frames that are accurate, positive, engaging, compelling, and healing.

Fourth: We need to have many—and sometimes surprising—voices at the table, especially marginalized voices. Women and youth and indigenous people and immigrants, differently abled people, poor people, and those who

have suffered trauma or discrimination all must be heard. Unless we are intentional about diversity of expression in the media and in our outcomes, we risk bland homogeneity on the one hand or strident extremism on the

> Include multiple (and sometimes unexpected) voices in decision making.

other. We must find ways for diverse voices to be heard. In the words of the old African proverb, "Until the lions can tell their own story, tales of the hunt will always glorify the hunter."

Finally, we must see the new thing that God is doing in our midst and seek paradigms that promote imagination, creativity, free expression. Perhaps imagination is the key—that human quality that still moves us to dare to dream, that emboldens us, that enables us to create new products and practices, that dimension of our heart and mind and soul that moves us to ever deeper understandings of ourselves, our world, and our God. If we can accomplish this, we can help ensure that our children and our children's children inherit a more peaceful world.

It is easy to expound upon lofty principles, but only as the concepts of mutual respect and understanding are expressed in day-to-day community life, can we succeed in changing the world.

10 | Generations

It is only with the heart that one can see rightly;
what is essential is invisible to the eye.[1]

—*Antoine de Saint-Exupery*

Have you ever been terrified? Truly terrified?

Our kids were little. We went for a brief vacation in New England and we stayed in a hotel that had a pool—a real treat for us. As I was watching our oldest daughter, Kristin, who was about seven and who could swim like a fish, jump off the diving board, our youngest—Kierra, who couldn't swim—was holding on to the side of the pool at my feet. "Dad, Dad . . . watch me dive," Kristin exclaimed. I looked up and watched as she jumped. It seemed like only a moment had passed, but when I looked down, Kierra had slipped from the side of the pool and was underwater, arms extended over her head. Fortunately, I was able to reach way down and pull her up by her outstretched arms, but for that brief instant, as I watched her beneath the water, it felt like my whole life was over. It lasted only an instant, though it seemed like an eternity. That eternal moment reminded me again about life's fragility and how we must live every second with the knowledge that it can never be repeated.

Echoes of this very personal story reverberated some months later while I was on my first international photographic shoot for a project I was doing for the Presbyterians. My colleague and friend, Cliff Aerie, and I had traveled to Nicaragua during the time of the Contra War. It was a really busy time in my life and much of what I learned about the country—its politics, its people, its geography—I learned on the spot. Nicaragua was, essentially, two countries, divided by the central highlands separating the higher, dryer west coast with its lighter-skinned, Catholic population from the wetter, lower lying east, inhabited by darker skinned Protestant people, including the Miskito Indians. The eastern part of Nicaragua is one of the wettest places on earth. At the time, no road went from west to east. Cliff and I had to drive overnight deep into the jungle to board a river boat that would take us to the east coast town of Bluefields, where we were scheduled to videotape a gathering of Moravian missionaries who were exploring ways to enhance the standard of living among the marginalized people in the eastern part of the country.

We left Managua late at night. The road left the high planes of Nicaragua's west coast and plunged into the darkest jungle I had ever experienced. We knew it was dangerous. The United States was in an undeclared war with the Sandinista government of Nicaragua. Though our trip was apolitical, Americans were not supposed to travel outside the commercial zone of Managua. Young and inexperienced, we didn't pay too much attention. In fact, it seemed more exciting than dangerous.

We were scheduled to meet a river boat at 6:00 AM in the remote town of Rama, where the road coming from the west literally ended. No more road; just jungle and river. Sometime in the middle of the night I saw violent death for the first time in my life. Our driver did not speak English and we did not speak Spanish, so I could not confirm it. But it was unmistakable. We had rounded a bend when suddenly the jungle darkness was punctuated with a scene I will never forget.

Out of nowhere, armed soldiers were standing in the middle of the road. At their feet, a man lying on the ground. He was in the most unnatural, awkward position, obviously dead. By the side of the road, women and children were huddled with their hands behind their heads. An ambush? Retribution? A political execution? I never learned. Cliff and I exchanged nervous glances. Our understanding of the danger in our situation rapidly escalated. We had no official documents. No one knew we were there. We could not speak the language. Our driver seemed to freeze up, looking straight ahead as we were waved through the hastily constructed checkpoint and continued on our way through the darkness. Cliff and I never spoke about it until later.

We were dropped off, promised that our transport to the east coast would arrive. The driver left. We were alone, waiting for the river boat to arrive. Between terror and amazement, we waited, unsure of where we were or if our contact would ever show up. No one knew we were there. It was more than a little unsettling. But sure enough, just before 6:00 AM, a boat appeared in the muddy harbor and we were taken downstream to the Atlantic coast. The boat trip was amazing in itself. We stopped for a "coffee break" where our captain went into the jungle and picked bananas and mangoes for the freshest snack I'd ever had. His small portable radio brought news of a record-setting snowstorm back home as we traveled downstream through the jungle. We were relieved to be in the light, having come through a night of uncertainty where we witnessed firsthand the violence of the then secret Contra War.

Terror takes many forms—some quite private; others scream out to us online or in the evening headlines. How we respond to terrifying situations, whether seeing a loved one in a life-threatening situation or being "behind the lines" in one of America's many undeclared wars, can shape the way we view the unfolding challenges of history and our role to make the world a better place. And the feeling of helplessness, if repeated regularly, can become psychologically debilitating to both individuals and whole communities. Such helplessness accentuates responses, sometimes in a destructive way.

One often overlooked aspect of our current reality is the cascading character of the information explosion that we so often take for granted. In Ray Kurzweil's book *The Age of Spiritual Machines*, the author maps the rate of technological advancement since time began and finds that the rate of change is not linear but exponential. Further, the concept of the singularity predicts the liberation of consciousness from the confines of human biology, allowing us not only to scale past the computational capacity of the human brain but also to interact directly with computer networks. We will become one with machines.[2]

Neural implants—which already exist—will enhance memory and correct personality disorders. Nanobots, robots designed on a molecular level, such as respirocytes—mechanical red-blood cells—will have myriad roles within the human body, including reversing human aging. Billions of nanobots in the capillaries of the human brain will create virtual reality from within the nervous system. You will be able to become a different person both physically and emotionally. Other people—such as your romantic partner—will be able to select a different body for you than you might select for yourself. The ethical implications of all this are overwhelming. And these developments are already occurring *at an exponential pace*.

To understand the impact of this, we need to remember the Chinese tale about the emperor and the inventor of chess. In response to the emperor's offer of a reward for his new beloved game, the inventor asked for a single grain of rice placed on the first square of the chess board. "Surely," the emperor said, "you must want more than that." "Yes," said the inventor, "I would like two grains of rice on the second square, four on the third, and so on."

The emperor quickly granted this seemingly benign and humble request. As the emperor and the inventor went through the first half of the chess board, things were fairly uneventful. The inventor was given spoons full of rice, then bowls of rice, then barrels. By the end of the first half of the chess board, the inventor had accumulated one large field's worth (four billion grains) and the emperor began to take notice. The second half of the board, sixty-three doublings, ultimately totaled eighteen million trillion grains of rice. At ten grains of rice per square inch, this required rice fields covering twice the surface area of the Earth, oceans included. It is in dispute which happened first: whether the emperor went bankrupt or the inventor lost his head.

But as Kurzweil points out, with regard to the doublings of computation, we currently stand about half way through the chess board: there have been slightly more than thirty-two doublings of performance since the first programmable computers were invented during World War II.[3]

"So what?" you may ask. "What has this to do with me?" Well, let's take my dad. I love my dad; I've known him all my life. A few years ago his hearing began to fail and he started wearing a hearing aid. No one would doubt that he is still my dad—just, my dad with a hearing aid. But then he needed a hip replacement. He's still my dad—now with a hearing aid and an artificial hip. Recently, he had a pacemaker put in to monitor his heartbeat. So, now he's my dad with a hearing aid, an artificial hip, and a pacemaker. But what if he has a neural implant to enhance his memory or change his personality? Or what if he has ten neural implants? Or a hundred, or a million? When does he cease being my dad—and who or what does he become?

On a crisp autumn day in 2012, my dad and I had a catch. There is nothing particularly remarkable in that. Except that, at the time, my Dad was ninety. We'd been having a catch for sixty years. How amazing is that?

The simple rhythm of tossing the baseball back and forth had opened channels of communication between us (as simple rhythms often do) for decades, and I wanted to capture what I knew would be one final time to savor the cadence of throw and catch, the whoosh of the ball moving through the air, the pop of it landing in the mitt: whoosh, pop, whoosh, pop. We reminisced (having a catch had always been a good time for reminiscing) while we were tossing the ball to one another—even at ninety, he still had a bit of a zip on his throw—about how we used to do the same thing, half a century ago; how he coached my Little League team; how we'd

Take the time, add a comma, have a catch.

play stickball in the street and shag flies in the school yard; how, on Labor Day, our extended family—uncles and cousins and various friends—could field two whole softball teams at our family's annual picnic at the state park near where we grew up.

When I was about eight, my dad took me to my first professional baseball game at the Polo Grounds in New York. I cheered when Alvin Dark hit an inside-the-park home run. It was in the days of black-and-white TV and I can still remember how radiant the field looked, so green and vivid, the uniforms in bright whites and blues instead of the shades of gray on the TV set. And I thought how this must be real while the rest of the world was but a shadow.

I thought what a blessing it was to have had my dad (and my mom!) with me for so long. They'd eventually pass their seventieth wedding anniversary in their own place, still driving (daytime only), entertaining, and performing multiple tasks in service to their family, their friends, and their community. Each has been a fount of wisdom and a constant support as I've tried to fill the world with those vibrant colors that I saw, maybe for the first time (while wearing my glasses of course) that day at the Polo Grounds.

The global issues that confront us in any given age—religious extremism, violence in the Middle East, workplace shootings, a deteriorating relationship between the United States and Pakistan, paralyzed and unresponsive government, millions out of work, dangerous shifts in climate, a quarter of our children at or near the poverty level, vitriolic political rhetoric, mass migration from countries ravaged by war and sectarian violence, the nagging unresolved sickness of racism that plagues out society, the breakdown between law enforcement personnel and the communities they serve—can easily overwhelm.

But on that sunny autumn day, I remembered that the baseball playoffs were in full swing and, as the ball went back and forth between my dad and me, it was easy to focus on life's most intimate blessings, to momentarily leave the world's suffering and anxiety behind, and to understand who we are and what we should strive to become. As I think about the global issues that confront us, it is important to return to those simple moments of appreciation for an autumn day having a catch with my dad in his ninety-first year. In an age of instantaneous communication that prompts ever more rapid responses, it is essential to add a comma and pause to savor the simple things that we too often take for granted, and to appreciate what lies beyond the comma. This is how we become whole.

Then, there is my mom.

Once, while at a conference in Kazakhstan, I had occasion to meet Bibi Russell, one of the world's rare treasures. Bibi was among the first supermodels in the 1970s to break the color barrier in the West. She appeared on the covers of *Vogue, Cosmopolitan* and *Marie Claire* and on runways in fashionable cities around the world. But, at the height of her success, she sacrificed it all and turned her attention to those from whom she drew her original inspiration: the artisan community of her native Bangladesh— mostly women—where she was introduced to colors, fabrics, and styles that captured her imagination.

Recognizing that the designs developed in these rural villages could both influence the world of fashion and generate income for the poor, she sought to connect these artisans with global markets as a way to improve their economic viability and give them voice. Bibi sacrificed a lucrative career on the world's fashion runways to provide work for tens of thousands of Bangladeshi women. Her business model has been replicated in India, Sri Lanka, Cambodia, Columbia, Spain, and other places where people understand that if women are lifted up, and art and craft can do that, then the whole of society benefits.

Intersections brought Bibi to New York as an example of—indeed, a personification of—what it means to be simultaneously a person of "power" and of "values." She received an "Urban Angel" award from New York Theological Seminary, appearing at a formal gala surrounded by wealthy and well-connected New Yorkers. On the global scale she teaches us that it is possible to engage in business for social change and that clothing and choices of fabric play an important role in supporting human rights. She has created jobs and dignity for thousands of indigenous women and other low-income individuals throughout the world.

At a more intimate dinner, the night before the gala, I asked Bibi what motivated her to do her work. She said that, when she was a child, she had a dream to give voice to all those women who struggled financially but who created magnificent fabric with their weaving and dye making. When she achieved the status that could enable her to empower others, she devoted herself tirelessly—forsaking personal comfort (she lives quite simply) so that others could improve their quality of life.

As for my mom—she has spent her life a world away from Bibi Russel, growing up on suburban Long Island, moving to different locations in the Northeast, basically following my father's vocational transfers—there are profound similarities with the Bangladeshi supermodel. Despite her relentless cooking and cleaning and arranging floral bouquets, despite raising four kids and managing a household in which, no matter what we did, my siblings and I always felt safe and secure, despite all she has sacrificed—she has never once made me feel obligated to return the favor. What an amazing quality to carry into the relationships that you generate over a lifetime.

> She never once made me feel obligated to return the favor.

There is no substitute for offering the example of a life well lived for your children to emulate, as my mother did, without expecting any return. But is there not also pressure on parents (and school teachers and clergy and community leaders) to provide proverbial wisdom so that the next generation can get a handle on how to live their lives? What do you tell your kids that will somehow change the way they view the world, the actions they take in treating others, what they leave behind for their own children?

Our eldest daughter, Kristin, was an exuberant child. She was always active, always inquisitive. Once when she was very young, I remember a neighbor volunteering to babysit. The neighbor had had four girls (including twins) in rapid succession, all just a little older than Kris. I remember picking her up late in the afternoon and how their living room looked like a disaster area—four little girls sprawled out exhausted all over the furniture and the rug, as if they had been hit by a delta strike force. Kristin, though, was bouncing about, running up and down the stairs, chattering away. She had, single-handedly, run her four friends into the ground.

It was time to try a quick proverbial piece of wisdom and so I summoned my most clever self and told her to always remember two things: share and be gentle. As she grew, I repeated this advice over and over in a variety of "teachable moments." Sometimes, I'd ask: what are the two things you must always do? And she would respond, "share and be gentle." It would be inaccurate to say that she went through her whole life with gentle generosity, but it is also remarkable how many times she has told me, even decades later, how this simple phrase had impacted her life. And each time she'd tell me signaled a personal success and was a quiet moment of pride that I had made a difference—however small—in the world.

> Share and Be Gentle

Do I take after my parents? Do my children take after me? My grandson, Nico, who is eight years old at this writing, has far more than a passing resemblance to me. Two occasions stand out: Once when he was about five, I was chaperoning his birthday party as a score of his peers whooped and hollered in the studio that is his parents' office—and a great place for kids to let off steam. One of his friends—mind you, he was about five—came up to me and said, "You must be Nico's grandfather, you look exactly like him." On another occasion, Nico was visiting my office at Intersections and, as we were leaving the building, the security guard looked at us and exclaimed, "Twins!"

What was interesting to me about these two incidents was the way these comments simultaneously made me feel proud and also filled with a kind of nostalgic regret. I know that as Nico grows, he will not remember these experiences. Indeed, I can only hope that he remembers me at all. But even though these comments were only based on our physical resemblance, I felt a deep connection that superseded my lifetime in what my Native American friends call the legacy of seven generations. I felt (and continue to feel) an intense pride about this intergenerational connection while wondering how his life will unfold long after (*in sha'Allah*) my life will be over. Is this what immortality means? And is it only in the limits of my imagination that I can conceive of, let alone influence, who and what he will become? Does it represent, even for him, being at a "thin place" between past and future, where we are connected not only to one another, but to all humankind and to the Creator of the Universe?

Parents mold and shape their offspring. This is certainly true in my case. I have been blessed with an extraordinary grounding that has had a direct impact on how I live my life. I am forever grateful for this. As I age, I recognize that increasingly those who fill my life are younger—sometimes much younger—as the previous story demonstrates. If I am truly attuned to my surroundings, it is clear I can learn valuable lessons from these interactions as well. If we are attentive to the flow of life around us, the stories that unfold in our day-to-day lives reveal poignant and profound intersections—things you can't make up, but that remind you of how holy moments interrupt our lives in real time and without warning.

Such an experience happened over Christmas vacation in 2013.

Intersections had recently moved to its new location on W. 28th Street. The floor of our office needed to be resurfaced and so just before Christmas we neatly boxed our supplies and stacked computers and furniture into one half of our facility, creating a warehouse environment in half of our space, while leaving the other half empty.

That afternoon, as the last of our staff departed for the holidays, my seven-year-old granddaughter, Sonoma, and I went on a shopping spree, gathering glittery branches and garland, peacock feathers, holiday balls and berries (28th Street is the heart of Manhattan's flower district) and then ascended to the eleventh floor to create a "magic forest" as a surprise gift for her parents on Christmas Day.

We carved out a space amidst the stacks of boxes and rows of file cabinets. Sonoma was so-o-o excited to be secretly creating this surprise, making up stories about the fairies that lived in the sparkly forest, their special powers to talk to animals, grant wishes, and heal hurts. Words cannot adequately convey the wonder of those brief moments for me, a transcendent time I will always cherish—just the two of us working on this joyful task as Sonoma's lively chatter washed over me. Our warehouse space was transformed into Santa's workshop.

On the day after Christmas, I learned that Intersections had been robbed. I made my way from my home in New Jersey to discover that the neat boxes our staff had stacked had been ransacked, office supplies and theatre costumes strewn on the floor and closet doors left ajar. Santa's workshop was in disarray. And in the empty half of the office, a single cigarette butt had been crushed on our shiny new floor.

Not much was taken, really. We saw video of the culprit's Christmas Day entry and his departure from the building. It took a while for the police to process their reports and do forensics, and while I waited their reports there was a lot of time for reflection. The feeling in the darkened room that held such joy just days before was more sad than ominous, the recognition that at the very time I was enjoying a Christmas feast with family and friends and Sonoma was presenting her magic forest to her parents, this man was rummaging through boxes alone looking for something to fill the emptiness of his life.

Things were eventually put right, the boxes emptied and the furniture returned to its rightful place on our resurfaced wooden floor. The staff anticipated the New Year's challenges before us, and our "warehouse space" had been cleaned and cleared in preparation of our first public presentations upcoming shortly after the first of the year.

The return to order in our offices masked the holy moments that happened over our holiday break—a space that saw the juxtaposition of unbounded joy with the realities of a city where life is often hard and lonely. I celebrate that brief time with Sonoma, with her soaring imagination and her eyes so alive with intensity on creating just the right look among the colors and textures of her magic forest. I grieve for the man who entered that sacred space, seeking some solace on Christmas Day. And I am reminded once again about the intersections, the thin places, in which we find ourselves—sometimes when we least expect it.

Sonoma is an individual acutely aware of both her surroundings and herself. Once when we were at a family outing, I complimented her on being so pretty and so intelligent and so well spoken. She quickly corrected me.

"I am something else," she said.

"What is that?" I asked.

"I'm also fierce."

I am sure even Sonoma missed the ironic juxtaposition of what had transpired that day just before Christmas. I am not even confident that she had a sense of the dynamics that this series of events evoked in me. But it is inaccurate to think that such moments do not cast a lasting impression on what matters to you as a unique individual.

For example, I have always assumed that, since I stand 6'8", it is essential to my sense of self that I am an excellent basketball player. While I did play in college at Duke, a perennial basketball powerhouse, even in the sixties, my dirty little secret is that my basketball career was less than a footnote. I played a total of twenty-three minutes as a college freshman and never after that. If someone drills down into my basketball career, I have all sorts of well-constructed caveats: I scored nineteen points in those twenty-three minutes (despite memory loss with advancing age, I can say that without hesitation: it is forged deeply into my consciousness!) I suffered a concussion in practice halfway through the season and did not play after that.

I transferred to University of Pennsylvania, where I played under Dick Harter, Chuck Daley, and Digger Phelps—three of the best coaches in history—and still I could not advance my career. After sitting out for the obligatory transfer year, I quit basketball because I found a more fulfilling future in the church. It's not a bad reason and the results proved that I made the right decision. But nothing I have done in my career—or ever will do—can erase the "small" matter of not living up to my basketball potential, simply because I was 6'8" and programmed to be great on the hardwood!

The depth of this power on my thought process can be seen in two incidents that occurred thirty years apart. In ninth grade—*ninth grade*— I was playing in my last game at Island Trees Junior High School in Levittown. I was about to move with my family to a larger house in a suburb further from the city. I was playing at the end of the game, which was close—we were down by two points. It was unusual for me to be playing in such an important moment since I was far from the best player on the team. Nevertheless, after a teammate took a shot, I rebounded the ball with all the gusto an insecure high school freshman can muster. I was fouled with seconds remaining. I stepped to the foul line to try to sink two foul shots that would tie the game. I missed them both. That was my final impression on the Levittown school system and the pain (guilt) of that loss haunted me deep into adulthood. Again, I was in ninth grade! There was seemingly nothing on the line. Still, for decades, I could not shake the negative feelings this "failure" evoked deep in my consciousness.

Thirty years later, I was in a pick-up league in rural upstate New York. We were playing for the championship in a tournament that no one knew or cared about. By then, I was in my mid-forties, still playing, still struggling with mediocre talent, added to now by advancing age, to make my basketball mark. We were not favored to win the game but we stayed close until

> Seemingly small incidents can have a powerful and lasting impact on behavior; tread gently on the histories of others.

the end when, with time expiring and the score tied, I was again fouled. Same scenario as three decades earlier. Only this time, I made both foul shots and we held on for the final seconds to grab a win.

Redemption! Though it took me thirty years and though neither game captured any media attention or was even noticed beyond a very small circle, I felt vindicated—exhilarated, even. I had rewritten that painful chapter in my personal history, I made the shots, the team won. It took thirty years but the sting of the loss in junior high school eased just a little bit in that moment. Small things, though our brains tell us they are inconsequential, can matter a great deal—enslaving or liberating us for reasons that may be too complex or too in-depth for us to examine rationally. But to assume that these events are unimportant totally misses the mark as to what it means to be human.

11 | Keep Talking

Most people do not listen with the intent to understand;
they listen with the intent to reply.[1]

—*Stephen R. Covey*

M uch of my vocational life has centered on communications. One helpful insight lies in understanding that all communications consist of four things: a transmitter, a receiver, a conduit, and "noise." My job is often to clearly identify who was transmitting information to whom, how the receivers were getting the message, and what might be in the way of a clear signal. No matter how elaborate the conversation, if these four elements are known and understood, information can be more easily clarified and discrepancies in communication more easily identified.

I learned this once as a pre-teen, back in my Levittown days. On one of those sultry summer afternoons when, as a ten-year-old, time seemed endless, a friend and I decided we'd make a telephone using tin cans and a string. And so we strung a long string—maybe two hundred feet—between his second-floor bedroom and mine and then went to bed for the evening, planning on holding subversive conversations (it was probably innocuous, though it seemed subversive because we were doing this on our own without parental knowledge or permission).

We both fell asleep and awoke the next morning to find that somehow the illicit conversation we had hoped to have had never occurred. What could have gone wrong? I was quick to blame the technology—it just didn't work. But much later I realized that we had strung our "conduit" resting against branches of a tree between our two bedrooms thereby rendering the communication pathway useless. Further, when my father came home from work that evening he reported that late at night he was checking on my siblings and me and he saw this random string that seemed to run from my night stand out the window. Not knowing what it was, he yanked it and the line broke. As I encountered communication challenges in the coming decades, I often thought about this pre-teen experience as I tried to unpack the complexities of our world's most pressing issues and how we might market them to a waiting world.

In matters large and small, one of the quickest roads to failure is to halt conversation. The more intimate the subject, the closer the characters in the dialogue, the harder the conversation. We can have endless discussions about faraway places and exotic people, but if the players in the conflict are family, friends, or close colleagues the conversation becomes increasingly more difficult.

A few years ago we hosted a panel discussion that featured three Iraqi men who had worked for the U.S. government during the war and who had to flee for their safety, relocating to the United States. One, Ehab (his last name was withheld out of fear of reprisals back home), told about his fear while being tortured in an Egyptian jail that he would be sent back to Iraq to be beheaded. Beheaded! This was before headlines about ISIS desensitized us all to this horrific act, and the only time I heard someone actually tell a personal story of his fear of beheading.

At the time, Ehab blamed people of faith for the fanaticism imbedded in the sectarian violence in his country. Later in the evening, during a question and answer session, he was asked about the racist treatment of Iraqis by U.S. soldiers, and again he blamed people of faith. But then he paused. After a moment's silence, he said that since having met Intersections staff and having encountered the work we are doing across lines of faith and culture to heal the suffering wrought by war, he was forced to reconsider that, while people of faith (in this case, Christians) can be grossly insensitive and destructive, those who base their ethical principles on their belief systems can also be kind and generous and good.

During a subsequent UPIC trip to Pakistan, we had moved to Lahore for the final two days of our gathering. A relatively uneventful trip (one bag lost) and some interesting conversations onboard during our brief flight led us to the campus of Lahore University of Management Sciences (LUMS), one of our sponsoring partners. This acclaimed school—sometimes called the Harvard of Pakistan—had a reputation for turning out some of the finest students in the country, many of whom go on to further studies in the United States. It was, therefore, a good place to get a toehold onto the conversation about how we might bridge the divides that exist between our two countries. But, even at LUMS, differences between Americans and Pakistanis were all too readily apparent.

We had been in conversation with students and faculty and community leaders, each of whom came to the gathering with a distinct worldview. Dr. Alan Jones, former dean of Grace Cathedral in San Francisco, used a helpful phrase as a reminder of what we were there to do. He called it the "lust for certainty" that keeps people apart. It is the fear brought on by the threatening quality we ascribe

Beware the "lust for certainty."

to the unknown, as we encounter "the other," that we must seek to overcome. Truly, as conversations unfolded, you could sense new ideas forming, new depths of understanding being realized, and respect growing.

Friendships were clearly being kindled. Charles Ramsey of Foreman Christian College in Lahore reminded us that building an ongoing community among ourselves was, in itself, no small task. "Stay the course" became a mantra—and a life lesson for us all. Even though the intensity of media coverage may rise and fall, even though tensions ebb and flow, our most effective strategy was simply to continue along the path to mutual respect and understanding—to keep meeting, no matter what was happening on the global stage.

When it comes to American foreign policy, we continue to get ourselves into no-win situations. The height of the unrelenting Syrian civil war provides a striking case in point. In 2013, there was seemingly incontrovertible evidence that the regime of Bashar al-Assad had used chemical weapons against the Syrian people, killing more than a thousand people, including four hundred children.[2] The video record of these heinous atrocities is gut-wrenching.

It is hard to believe, especially with the insipid denials of culpability that came from Damascus, that this attack was not sanctioned at the highest levels of the Syrian government. Assad had crossed President Obama's "red line" as well as international "rules of war." If this action went without consequences, the administration argued, our "word" would lose its credibility on the global stage.

How, then, were we as a nation to appropriately respond? We were weary of war. We did not want to risk American lives and property for civil strife in another land. Yet, was it not incumbent upon us to be responsible global citizens? If the UN's Security Council would not act, could we avoid the role of holding world leaders to standards of behavior upon which virtually all civilized nations agree? If not us, then who? If not now, when? And what is our role as individuals within this complex conflict?

Domestically, one argument was that the President must seek congressional approval. Keeping Congress accountable for acts of war is a critical constitutional principle and its role in contemporary declarations (or not) of war has been significantly reduced in recent conflicts. A clear up-or-down vote by representatives could help the American people understand where our elected officials stand on this important issue, thereby clarifying the position we would take on individual legislators and strengthening our democracy. But failing such a vote, how do we as individuals express our thoughts on this or other crises with global implications?

It is the President who is both commander-in-chief and communicator-in-chief and who is ultimately responsible for whatever course of action the United States would take on this or any of a host of other policies. The complexities of the issue are immense: political dysfunction domestically; the rise of ISIS, Al-Nusra Front, Al-Qaeda, and other terrorist forces in the Syrian opposition; the balance of power in the Middle East; the impact of all this on Israel; and Iran's nuclear program all factor into the decision-making.

Two things I lament—elements that the Syrian predicament laid out in stark relief. First, military intervention continues to be the default position for us as a nation. We say it is a last resort, but we run there too quickly. Our government must find other avenues for peacemaking and then invest in those efforts with time, resources, personnel, energy, and imagination so we do not continue to find ourselves boxed into corners where the only way out seems to be through military intervention. If we invested similar resources in *seeking* peaceful solutions, we might actually *find* peaceful solutions to these seemingly intractable issues between nations.

Second, by fostering conversations in safe spaces, involving diverse and unexpected participants, where people build relationships over time *before* untenable situations arise, we might uncover bold and innovative solutions to the world's problems. But we seem to be afraid to construct these "open tables" in the public square where a variety of viewpoints can be shared. Do we fear loss of face, the appearance of weakness or naiveté, that we will be duped by scurrilous adversaries, that our domestic political foes will attack us? Truth is, if we had spoken as resolutely about the open tables we need as we did about the red lines that could not be crossed, perhaps the conversations, and subsequent actions, would have evolved quite differently.

Few of us can pretend to know all the geopolitical specifics that need to go into an informed decision about the nature of our response as a nation to these events. But can the decision-making process itself teach us lessons—both positive and negative—about our interpersonal relationships and how we address decision making at very personal levels? Like our nation, we as individuals often run to the "fight" option too quickly. We are inconsistent in creating safe space for conversations and we are too limited—and limiting—in who we include in the conversations once they take place.

It is essential that we "keep talking." Two things happen: we continue to learn from the other—be they friend or adversary—and, hence, new "framing," and new initiatives and approaches can emerge; and, as long as we are in dialogue with "the other" it is far more difficult to engage in violence with the other. This is not only true in the geopolitical arena, but serves as an important principle for small communities as well—extended families, work colleagues, close friends. As we keep talking, the frames we use to shape our realities continue to shift, offering the possibility for new understandings and compromise.

> Keep talking and be attentive to framing.

Why would framing matter? I am reminded of the story of a cellist in Sarajevo who, in the midst of the Balkan Wars, took his instrument into the town square and set up his chair. As bombs were falling all around, he began to play. A reporter, sensing a great story, dodged the raining shrapnel, raced up to him, and asked, "Why are you out here playing your cello while they're dropping bombs?" The cellist looked at the reporter and asked with indignation, "Why are they dropping bombs while I'm playing my cello?" Changing the frame makes all the difference.

We must listen to one another, whether we are nine or ninety, to create safe space. Do not be afraid to express your thoughts, tell your story, and address one another without suspicion, rather, assuming the best of intentions. Be patient. Be generous. Approach the tasks ahead that come with being God's people in love and grace and forgiveness.

Acknowledgment is key. There's a great hunger in our world to find places where our voices can be heard, our stories honored, and where we can make authentic connections that deepen our experience of community. Only as we live interdependent lives can we gain the empathy needed to make sustained change in ourselves and in our world. Only then can we truly be independent of the forces of greed and exclusion that surround us so that we might fully experience life's abundance.

> Acknowledgment is key.

And one more thing: don't think that, if you forget to offer acknowledgement in the moment, the opportunity has passed forever. It is never too late to offer thanks and praise. Rarely do we ever feel that we are acknowledged too much. And in a day when the means of communication—e-mail, Facebook, Twitter, Snapchat, etc.—are multiple and varied and easily accessible, there is always an opportunity to say "nice job" or "thank you" after the fact . . . even years after the fact.

There are structured events that provide this opportunity—family gatherings, high school reunions—but these events don't carry the same power as individual expressions for no apparent reason. My life has been liberally seasoned with individuals who contact me without prior notice to offer a grateful story about how I have positively influenced their life. Sometimes these stories are from interactions that are years old. Inevitably, such expressions leave me with a positive feeling and evoke fond memories of the time in question. If that is true for me, why should it not be true when I share such positive feelings, even belatedly, with others? What are we waiting for?

12 | Intersections

I like to say that I'm tracing the intersection between big ideas and human experience, between theology and real life.[1]

—*Krista Tippett*

Do you remember the proverbs of your childhood? A stitch in time, saves nine. You can't tell a book by its cover. Children should be seen and not heard. (How'd you feel about that one?) If you can't say something nice about someone, don't say anything at all. (Sounds like the Internet—we wish!) Only you can prevent forest fires. Don't talk to strangers.

These are "wisdom sayings" that we heard as children. Many of them have their roots in the Book of Proverbs; indeed, there is a whole genre of wisdom literature in the Bible—in Proverbs, Ecclesiastes, Job, Song of

Songs, the Psalms, and some of the prophetic writings that call on us to believe God's word and to live with righteousness, not seduced by the ways of the world.

A specific childhood proverb comes to mind, one that forms the opening words of the prologue to this book: "Cross at the green and not in between." Although biblical proverbs have a whole different context from this childhood lesson, the connection resonates. "Wisdom" in Hebrew is always personified as a woman. In the ancient verses in Proverbs 1:20–21, "Wisdom cries out in the street; in the squares she raises her voice. At the busiest corner she cries out; at the entrance of the city gates she speaks." Wisdom cries out not only in the street, but at the busiest corner—at the intersection. And this, I contend, is where we find the most important lessons of our faith: not among the power elite or those who have celebrity status; not in the hallowed halls of our academic institutions; not even in the sacred space of our sanctuaries. It is in the streets and, more pointedly, at the intersection.

It is here we can learn about wisdom, from the Korean grocer and the homeless vet, from the family living in their car and the banker passing by without noticing, from the #BlackLivesMatter protester and the high-priced lawyer, from the woman on welfare and the street kid in baggy pants, from the wrongly accused and the routinely abused, from the Muslim on his way to prayers and the Pentecostal street preacher raising his voice above the din, from the cross dresser and the genuflector, from the sex worker and the shop keeper. This is the crucible of life. Lessons abound.

My favorite New York story: I was walking near our Intersections office recently and I came upon a couple walking and animatedly talking to each other. He was jet black, sculpted body, dressed like he had just stepped out of a photo shoot for GQ. She was equally beautiful, like a Swedish goddess with long blond hair and impossibly long legs. As I came up behind them, I thought to myself—this is what I love about New York, people who are so different coming together, engaging one another face-to-face in the things that make for everyday life—and then I realized that they were speaking Japanese.

Important and surprising
lessons are learned
on the streets.

This quick experience epitomizes the wisdom of the streets. I thought I had the story all figured out—beautiful, interracial couple—and if I had seen this from an office window, I would have missed the clincher—their interracial relationship, whatever it was, was beside the point. Appearances did not matter. They were communicating across cultures in an unexpected language. *That* lesson I could only learn by being on the streets.

Where are the safe spaces so we can talk together across lines of faith and culture? What are the civic sectors that can build bridges by telling the truth and honoring "the other"? Our political candidates play fast and loose with the truth. Our governments are dysfunctional. Our corporations race to the bottom line. The media? Networks and newspapers are more concerned with profits than they are with prophets.

The Internet and social networks do not reveal the truth but rather nudge us into corners inhabited by like-minded souls. Though we have greater capacity than ever to know about the nuances of our world, we tend to hang with those who think like us. A message may be slicker or louder or generate more traffic, but that doesn't make it true, and it doesn't make it right and it doesn't make it just and it sure as hell doesn't make it honorable.

Today's technology offers the opportunity for anyone to put anything online and have it travel across the landscape with lightning speed. Kittens playing pianos have a huge following and a failed Protestant preacher can promote an amateurish video with production values so poor it wouldn't pass muster in your average high school media club, and yet it gains a worldwide audience and a geopolitical impact that leads to violence and even death. Duke University's Bruce Lawrence said this in Religious Dispatches about the Benghazi tragedy:

Beyond all the issues that have been discussed, debated, and fine-tuned since the 9/11/12 tragedy in Benghazi, one central point has been missed, and it needs to be made again and again and again: expect the unexpected, look for the unrelated to be connected, then projected.[2]

For me, offering someone a job has always been a sacred trust. As director of various entities throughout my career, I have often been in a position to hire. The act of hiring gives me great joy—both empathetically for the one hired, but also for the opportunity to work on important issues in succeeding months and years. But the downside of this equation lies in the fact that is has

> Expect the unexpected.

also been my responsibility on numerous occasions to terminate someone, often a person that I have worked with closely for a long time. No matter how the termination process is undertaken, it is never pleasant and invariably exacts a heavy emotional toll not only on the one being let go, but also on me. In November of 2016, I was in that very position on the day that the results of the 2016 presidential election became clear.

I was also in the midst of my manuscript for this book. It struck me how the premise upon which this narrative is based had become so strikingly apparent. There I was, engaged in deep emotional turmoil about this very personal termination process when suddenly the collective fear and grief, sadness and recrimination that followed the surprise announcement of Donald Trump being elected President of the United States shattered the progressive community that so dominates New York City. Friends were weeping; the city seemed in mourning; protesters spontaneously emerged on the streets of cities across the country within hours of the results being announced.

How do these two elements connect? What can I learn from the intersection of this very personal struggle that impacts lives of people who are close to me, against a political reality that has far-reaching, even generational, impact? What is my "true north" under such circumstances and how could I be attentive to my

> What is your true north?

own internal emotional dynamics while also responsive to the urgent social and political realities that had just so unexpectedly erupted?

Before making a presentation to a gathering of human resources (HR) professionals, I had been struck reading an Urban League study about how negatively people felt about diversity training.[3] Overwhelming majorities saw the need for having a diverse work force, for reaching new and varied markets. Most thought they could function in a diverse work force, but the majority was dissatisfied with the efforts of their companies or organizations to ensure diversity or to equip people of color and women to rise through the power structure and into executive positions. There seemed to be a lack of trust in the professionals to get this important job done right. My personal anecdotal experience bore this out.

While I was at the United Church of Christ, an entity renowned for its commitment to social justice and an organization that put considerable resources, time, and dollars into antiracism and diversity training, employees fiercely believed that those efforts were woefully unsuccessful. Judging from the Urban League study, the United Church of Christ was not alone. So why is it so hard to get this right? Why, if we all believe that diversity in the workplace is good for both the individual and the company, are our efforts to ensure this critical aspect of our strategic organizational plans so uneven? Are there things—obvious things—that we are just missing? Are there similar blind spots in our personal relationships?

> We have been conditioned by generations of tribal warfare to view "the other" as suspicious, even hostile.

Three things come to mind. First, we have been conditioned by generations of tribal warfare to view "the other" as suspicious, even hostile, often for no other reason than they are simply not the same as us. From Kosovo to Kenya we see how differences that seem unrecognizable to outsiders create separation and violence when played out against centuries of animosity.

Second, we are all suspicious of things that seem to come from the top.

Third, despite the notion that "random acts of kindness" abound in our vocational and avocational relationships, life in the trenches is more competitive than we would choose to believe, and we tend to operate out of a context—perceived or imagined—of scarcity rather than abundance.

So, what can HR professionals and others do to develop a diversity plan that will be respected by the work force, and how do these forces impact our interpersonal relationships and the ways in which we behave towards one another? Are there lessons we can apply to our lives? I believe there are.

First, *be genuine.* HR professionals and other executives responsible for creating a healthy workforce must get in touch with and then "own" their prejudices, not being afraid to admit to blind spots. Staff will sniff out racism or sexism or homophobia in a heartbeat, so it does no one any good to try to hide it. Owning your own "isms" doesn't in itself construct an effective diversity plan, but it does let your colleagues know that we are all part of this problem. So, too, in our personal relationships: keep it real.

> Be genuine.

Second, *work hard at creating safe space.* It is within such an environment that women, people of color, people with disabilities, religious minorities, returning veterans, and other often marginalized groups can begin to talk about what separates them as well as what unites them. *Only* within a safe space can these issues be addressed in any great depth. If employees feel positive about the ways that management is investing in creating safe space, the ground has been ploughed to claim a positive response for a diverse work force and the training needed to increase the prospects of success in such an environment.

> Create safe space.

Third, honor and live out the mantra that *diversity rewards and is its own reward.* Make available opportunities for people to experience how diversity plays out in our society. Extravagant welcome is vital. Nurture relationships, networking, emersion experiences, and play. Use the arts to emphasize, demonstrate, and engage this principle. View the Oscar winning film *Crash*, and then talk about it.

Fourth, *language is critical*. View your plan through multiple lenses for insensitivities and outright mistakes. One incident comes to mind: We were about to include a Japanese gift-giving gesture in a public program we were doing. We had the program reviewed by an Asian staff member who said that the particular ritual we were planning to use was very sacred in Japanese thought and would be out of place—even offensive—in our setting, despite our best intentions. It is necessary to have antennae out for the systemic "isms" (racism, sexism, gender identity discrimination, homophobia, age discrimination, etc.) that can cause damage in interpersonal relations when it is least expected. Program initiatives, policy guidelines, and procedures in the workplace or among partners should be vetted through a variety of lenses so that blind spots (which can never be totally eliminated) are minimized.

Fifth, remember that at the end of the day, these issues boil down to two people sitting over a desk, often with someone's livelihood on the line—either as a recruit or as someone hoping for a promotion or dreading termination. *Treat potentially volatile moments with tenderness.* A rule of thumb that has been helpful for me has been to "think the best first." Rather than assuming that a colleague or counterpart has the worst intentions in mind, presume that she or he hopes for the best for you and then strive to clarify communication in order to work through differences. By assuming the best first, you can often avoid misunderstandings altogether.

> Think the best first and treat potentially volatile situations with tenderness.

One aside that is particularly relevant here has to do with communicating through e-mail or text messaging. Electronic means of communication—while often the most convenient way of connecting—do not allow for the nuance that comes through context, speech inflection, or body language. If I send a text when I am tired or distracted by something altogether different from my message, it is easy for you to read my distraction into the message, causing you to totally misconstrue my intent. By intentionally infusing tenderness into every interchange and considering each interaction as a sacred exchange, we can minimize the differences between us and avoid unnecessary misunderstanding and hostility. Given the rapid pace of communications in our contemporary world, this is not always a "given" and requires significant discipline.

It is important to remember that *true dialogue is hard*, especially around issues that have far-ranging social impact. It requires patience and often follows a circuitous path. It is important to keep talking, even when you are exhausted and feel like little progress is being made. An important element in a constructive dialogic process is active listening. This concept is so easily overlooked; but without empathetic listening, there is no real dialogue—merely a series of pronouncements made in a vacuum, with little possibility of sparking sustained change. One key arena in which seemingly endless conversations have been markedly unsuccessful in American society has been in the area of race relations.

So let's talk about race.

13 | Race

We look at young black kids with a scowl on their face,
walking a certain way down the block with their sweatpants
dangling, however, with their hoodies on. And folks think
that this is a show of power or a show of force. But I know,
because I've been among those kids, it ultimately is fear.[1]

—Ta-Nehisi Coates

graduated from New Brunswick Theological Seminary in 1972. It was a
different time then: the end of an era known as "the sixties," a time of
dramatic changes in the church, a time when the Vietnam War was still
raging. One of the issues that confronted the church then, as it does now,
is the distance between the clergy and the laity. I wanted to make a symbolic
statement in my senior year that I would be "with the people" and so I decided not to wear a robe—at my graduation, in my senior picture, in the
early days of my ministry. No robe.

Forty years later, and still: no robe, no collar, just a suit jacket. The symbolic statement I made decades earlier had become part of my liturgical practice ever since. Until the Sunday in early spring of 2012 when I removed my suit jacket and put on a hoodie in honor of Trayvon Martin and what his story should mean to all of America.

I had a sermon prepared, even held up the manuscript to prove my point. "I think it was pretty good," I said, not really sure if it was false modesty or for dramatic emphasis. The text for the morning had been the Lazarus story and I had spent extra time doing research, following the biblical narrative as it meandered through John's Gospel like a Gabriel Garcia Marquez novella, consuming more than fifty verses and all of chapter 11.

I focused not on the central hub of the story—the raising of Lazarus from death—but on its many meaningful spokes: the tensions or *intersections* between safety and danger; between allegiance to family and close friends and the call to serve the public; between *kairos* time and *chronos* time; the revealing conversation between Martha and Jesus; the role of those who just had to go tell the Pharisees about this to protect their place in society; and the devastating results of their striving for self-protection.

I saw in this circuitous narrative many clues as to how we should live our lives and then I made the obligatory connections to Intersections. It would have preached, no doubt. But sometimes, things happen that are so compelling, so instructive, that we must jettison our plans and respond to God's unfolding history in our midst. The emerging reality surrounding the death of Trayvon Martin was just such a time. President Obama had even weighed in, saying that this was personal; that if he had a son, the son would look like Trayvon. I knew it was personal, too, for many in the multiracial congregation. I shuddered to think how many "driving while black" or "walking while Latino" stories existed in the sanctuary.

Fact is, the Trayvon Martin story was personal for me too. I have an African American stepson whom I helped raise from middle school through college. Rhakeem graduated from Keane College in New Jersey, where he played tight end, and later became a police officer in Englewood, New Jersey. The thing about Rock is that he has a heart of gold and a body like Samson. His arms are bigger around than my thighs. One of my favorite pictures of him is when he was in college holding our infant nephew barely a few months old, his massive brown shoulders cradling the defenseless pink baby.

Under other circumstances, Rock might have been a prime target in a state with a "stand your ground" law that allowed someone to shoot a person they felt was intimidating them—Rock could intimidate you just by standing in front of you. But then he'd smile and you were totally disarmed, your fears melted, and you felt more than a little foolish. Fortunately, this combination of strength and gentleness is defending the public in Englewood. Thanks be to God.

But Rhakeem's life causes one to wonder: what good might Trayvon have done, had he lived? Would he have become a teacher, scientist, preacher, cop, dad, Marine, dancer? The profound personal tragedy in this story is that we will never know.

But there is more. If we ignore the convergence of the individual story with the broader social reality, if we stick purely to the personal, we miss the more universal truth about who we are as a people and how Trayvon's death became another statistic—yet another young black male sacrificed to the God of racism because of our blindness and insensitivity, and our unwillingness to pay the price to change the world. This reality was repeated with horrific regularity in 2015 and beyond as headline after headline screamed about yet another young black male being killed by law enforcement.

So, let's be clear, I went on to say in my sermon, about the lessons to be learned from this incident: this was about race. Trayvon was a black kid walking in a gated community in Florida. The police immediately sided with the shooter—can you imagine?—focusing the investigation on Trayvon and failing to collect forensic evidence at the scene or on the perpetrator. Trayvon's death became a marker for the #BlackLivesMatter movement that was soon to emerge, where the fear, frustration, and far-too-often tragic outcomes of police/community fragmentation was given voice.

The lesson: The senseless toll that racism takes on our society must end and we must end it wherever we may be. *We* must nip it in the bud. If we hear a racist comment, *we* must correct it—be it from a family member, a member of our congregation, a friend, or a colleague at work. If we see discrimination in the workplace, report it; if we catch a public official in a racist act, call it out. Enough is enough. We have the power to change this. Sometimes it involves action —difficult, controversial action; and we are called—each of us—to take those actions in order to ensure that this plague on our society comes to an end.

We must nip racism in the bud. If we hear a racist comment, correct it. If we see discrimination in the workplace, report it. If we catch a public official in a racist act, call it out.

Which brings me back to the Lazarus story. The story demands our attention, because it is at that critical intersection between life and death—both for Lazarus and for Jesus. The raising of Lazarus largely defines us as Christians—in Jesus Christ, the Gospel writer is saying, we have the power to overcome even the most significant obstacles—even death itself—so that nothing can keep us from God's love.

When Jesus first learns about the death of Lazarus, he stays for a while in the place where he is and then goes to Bethany, which immediately creates a stir among the disciples. They are sure that he will be persecuted. "The disciples said to him, 'Rabbi, the Jews were just now trying to stone you, and are you going there again?' Jesus answered, . . . 'Our friend Lazarus has fallen asleep, but I am going there to awaken him'" (John 11:8–11).

In seminary, I learned about the difference between *chronos* time and *kairos* time; *chronos* time is the linear ticking of the clock, measured in days, weeks, months, millennia. *Kairos* time is God's time—when God breaks into the universe to qualitatively shift the course of human events.

For Christians, Jesus' life is the most dramatic example of *kairos* time and, for Jesus, this journey to Bethany indicates why: there was an appointed hour for him to complete his ministry. His time was not yet up.

Raising Lazarus was the seventh of the miraculous signs in Jesus' ministry[2]—the culminating moment for him to fulfill the promise God made to humankind to show that nothing, not even death, could separate us from God's love. And, yet, Jesus interrupted his journey towards destiny to attend to his friendships with Mary, Martha, and Lazarus, offering healing—both physically and emotionally. This is the most dramatic "intersection" between the deeply personal and the universal in all of Christian scripture. The world could wait; Jesus' friend needed him. What does this say to us about how we are to prioritize our lives? And what does it tell us about the importance of interrupting our worldly obligations for seemingly small acts of kindness for those we are closest to? Do it!

> If a loved one needs you, the world can wait.

It was Memorial Day weekend in 2015, and I was investing considerable time on the subject of community policing, especially following events in Cleveland, the place I used to call home. Over that particular weekend, police officer Michael Brelo had been acquitted in the deaths of two unarmed African Americans, Timothy Russell and Melissa Williams, who were shot to death in November of 2012. These events, coupled with the fact that Intersections would be performing several staged readings of our latest production, *Uniform Justice*, in Cleveland at the end of June, compelled me to pay attention.

Uniform Justice is a play about an urban neighborhood where community members and police search for solutions to the violence that afflicts their streets and the conflicts and suspicions that divide them. Set in Memphis, Tennessee, and inspired by true stories, *Uniform Justice* came to Cleveland at a pivotal time during both local and national conversations on police/community relations. With its creative exploration of multiple experiences and perspectives, *Uniform Justice* serves as a unique vehicle to foster constructive dialogue on a pressing and polarizing current issue. *Uniform Justice* moves beyond superficial conversation and encourages deep and meaningful connections in the search for change, healing, and justice.

Circulating through the crowd following the first staged reading of the play, the most common word I heard among law enforcement and city officials in attendance was the word "real," referring to the trap of retaliatory violence—often originating as disputes among friends or family members—that afflicts so many lives in our urban areas and, increasingly, in our suburbs as well.

Using the arts to expose and articulate issues of social justice is a core aspect of Intersections' work, and *Uniform Justice* serves as a great example of how "keeping it real" can lead to constructive community dialogue and, ultimately, to policy prescriptions that change the way our society functions. Too often, such conversations are superficial or absent altogether.

Uniform Justice is a program that both law enforcement personnel and community members find meaningful. Based on a technique called "Insight Theatre," *Uniform Justice* seeks to move audiences "from judgment to curiosity," embracing the sentiments behind #BlackLivesMatter, while also affirming that "blue lives matter"[3] and that unless and until we can find respect for all, any healing in our nation's urban areas will be incomplete.

Our desire to offer the city of Cleveland a program that was appreciated by law enforcement personnel *and* community residents alike did not mean that we could or should overlook incidents of violence against people of color in our communities and seek ways to reduce them. That 137 rounds were fired into the car driven by Russell and Williams seems unacceptable under any circumstances. I found one element of Michael Brelo's testimony particularly troublesome.

According to *The Washington Post*, "Brelo fired his Glock 17 from his driver's seat, reloaded and emptied a second 17-round magazine. . . . He exited his car . . . to get to a safer position behind another squad car. A state investigator who interviewed Brelo after the incident testified that Brelo said he *drew on his Marine training* [italics mine] to 'go to an elevated position and push through the target.' Brelo stepped onto the hood of the Malibu, where he fired 15 shots into the windshield."[4]

The militarization of our law enforcement community is more than disconcerting; it is dangerous. Military training engages "targets" who are enemies and who seek to destroy the opposition. This is rarely the case on the streets of our country, and employing tactics similar to a war zone is a doomed strategy on many levels. Any substantive conversation between police and community needs to draw the sharp distinction between these two settings, a distinction that must be an integral part of "reintegration training" for members of our armed forces. Keeping clear the disparity between U.S. civilians and enemy combatants can make the difference between life and death and minimize the tendency toward violence that was spiraling out of control at that moment in our nation's history.

Shortly after the horrific tragedy in June 2015 at Emanuel AME Church in Charleston,[5] we were performing *Uniform Justice* in an all-black congregation in Queens, New York. The hall—which would ultimately hold more than seventy—was filling up nicely. My role was to introduce the show and so I waited in the rear of the house for my cue as last-minute arrivals filed into the few remaining empty seats. Suddenly, in walked a solitary, young white male, casually dressed, a baseball cap perched backward on his head. He sat by himself in the last row, spoke to no one, and waited quietly for the show to start.

Given the events of just a few days earlier, my imagination flew to the images of Dylann Roof, the Charleston shooter, and I couldn't help but take pause. What was this white kid doing here? The audience was virtually all black—families, elderly church people, a few young professionals—as was our *Uniform Justice* cast. To say he "stood out" was an understatement and for a moment I wondered—panicked is too strong a word; concerned would be more accurate—about his background, his motives for being there, his connection to the venue, how he had learned about the performance.

My concerns, of course, were ridiculous. He was a work colleague of one of our cast members, was enthralled by the story behind our performances, participated in the ensuing facilitated dialogue, and ended up traveling with a couple of us from the company back home on the bus and subway.

Later reflection, though, prompted a much deeper reminder, causing me to think about media stereotypes, about the experience of people of color in our society and the subtle and too often not-so-subtle ways that the racial constructs we have created in America have a devastating impact on so many lives. This young white male had "fit the profile" of the racist terrorist who had just taken nine innocent black lives in South Carolina—and yet here I was making instant judgment about him based on this profile and the media reporting that followed—not on anything about him as a person.

The fact that my concerns passed quickly did not minimize the initial impact that my own susceptibility to these media images had created in my head. How many millions of times over is this incident replicated in the consciousness of African American and Latino individuals, especially our youth—who are so often the ones targeted by media stereotypes as being "other" or "untrustworthy" or "dangerous"? And what is the long-term psychological damage done to individuals inadvertently caught in this media-fabricated web?

Part of the conversation about race that was prompted anew by the events in South Carolina, and similar events that subsequently ensued, must include the concept of white privilege and the clear acknowledgment that the experience of people of color in our country is different from that of whites. As a white person, I am part of what has been determined (who determined this, actually?) as the "societal norm." This means that (just because of my race) I am judged as an individual. There is, because of this systemic racism, an additional layer in judging a person of color, even if the context is complimentary: "He is a successful black man" (in spite of his race? having overcome his race? *because* of his race?); whereas I am simply "successful."

Constant qualifiers that society places upon people of color (even the former President of the United States) are signs that we have much still to discuss in any in-depth conversation about race. The solution, if there is one, is to keep talking, to keep building bridges—cultural, religious, lifestyle and, of course, racial—so that the "otherness" of the other does not disappear into a sea of homogeneity, but becomes a cause of celebration and a quality to embrace.

And yet, when I despair, I flash back to standing on a long line outside an old Episcopal Church in Jersey City in the pre-dawn light of November 4, 2008. I watched people coming from every direction to join that line— students and factory workers, young people and old, in sweat suits and business suits, people of every color and ethnicity—on their way to vote.

There was a quiet confidence palpable in the early morning stillness that later that night would erupt into jubilation from Times Square to Grant Park. It was a confidence that we as a society could move beyond the self-destructive boxes we had put ourselves into for so long to forge a new era of hope and cooperation. The phrase "the art of the possible" took on new meaning. We could dream again. We could once again rigorously exercise the muscles of our imaginations. We could reach across boundaries of politics and faith and culture and class and national borders to create new ways of relating.

There was a sense, for me, that we were witnessing what an old priest friend of mine calls *a very thin place*—when the divine spirit and the human spirit coexist in exceptionally close proximity. It is not about any particular candidate—actually I think President Obama's gift was his ability to discern this reality before the rest of us and he took advantage of a great longing in our society. It was, instead, a signature time in the human condition.

At these thin places, we experience anew what it means to be alive, to be fully present in history, to remember both pain and blessings of the past and think creatively and expansively about the future; and in the process, the distance between the real world and the spirit world, between the moment and the eternal, between the personal and the collective narrows, prompting us to confront the question, "What else can we accomplish"?

Live at the intersection; be the change you seek.

It didn't all work out as many of us had hoped—though some of it did. The scary, relentless drone of our inhumanity to one another continues to keep us isolated, arrogant, hurtful, and afraid. But, in the light of the gauzy hopefulness of that early November morning in 2008, building on a lifetime of love and support from family and friends, the challenge of creating a just world became even more important. It is an acknowledgement that we are called to be collaborators, incubators, conveners, and change agents.

We are to look for transformation within the individual and within society at large, to work with like-minded groups and individuals not to reinvent the wheel, but to deepen relationships, fill gaps, and build bridges. We are to bring people together who look at the world through different lenses so that new ways of problem solving might emerge. We are to explore radically new ways of thinking that lift people and organizations out of their silos and into a collaborative, synergistic model of relating, in the hope that the sand piles that have led to destructive behavior between us can dissolve in an avalanche of newness.

14 | Truth

You may shoot me with your words,
You may cut me with your eyes,
You may kill me with your hatefulness,
But still, like air, I rise[1]

—*Maya Angelou*

Social healing has been at the core of my professional life—whether it was as pastor of the Presbyterian Church of Teaneck, a multicultural congregation with no ethnic majority; or in my travels to remote locations for Creative Connections (a marketing/communications company I founded in the late 1980s, located in upstate New York), where I had the privilege of lifting up the stories of unknown "saints" who toiled in rural villages and urban slums; or in the UCC's identity campaign, whose core message was "no matter who you are or where you are on life's journey, you're welcome here"; or at Intersections in healing the rift between Muslims and non-Muslims or addressing the military/civilian divide or community policing, or standing alongside our collegiate and interfaith partners in prayer and outrage over the kidnapping of Nigerian schoolgirls. The phrase we frequently used for a time at Intersections as part of our logo, "Change Starts Here," was emblematic of the core of this principle.

Social healing involves taking stands that are uncomfortable at best, and can even be dangerous. I was in Pakistan in 2012, and for the first time I was able to move beyond the boundaries of our host institution, the Lahore University of Management Sciences. I was to meet with officials at the University of Management and Technology, a school that would eventually become a partner with us in this effort. But this was my first visit and, typical of Pakistani hospitality, we were invited to dinner.

However, before the meal was served, my colleague Eduardo Vargas and I were ushered into a separate boardroom where we were met by a couple dozen officials, mostly dressed in traditional garb, who proceeded to interrogate us to be sure of our intentions. At the time, I thought of media images of the *loya jirga*, local gatherings of elders in Afghanistan who came together to choose a new leader in times of crisis, invariably portrayed by American media as having sinister intent. While we were not exactly fearful, there was a level of intimidation in the room, and the differences between us did make for an uncomfortable encounter.

As lead spokesperson for our tiny group, I answered their questions as best I could, speaking about interreligious cooperation in the United States and how we wished to extend those efforts into Pakistan. I told our hosts that we were there to build relationships and end the cycle of mistrust that so negatively impacts our cross-border relations. Silent nods of approval filled the room; things seemed to be going well. Then, a man at the far end of the table said, "You are right that there is great room for cooperation between Christians and Muslims, but we both know that the real problem in our world lies with the Jews."

That is not my experience.

It was one of those moments when an immediate decision was called for. I could talk around the question and not offend my hosts or I could address the issue squarely and let the chips fall where they may. I chose the latter. My response was gentle but firm. "That is not my experience. I know many Jews who are deeply committed to interreligious cooperation, including outreach to the Muslim community. In fact, there have been Jews working with us in our outreach to Pakistanis. On this, then, we will simply have to respectfully agree to disagree."

Silence followed. Though it was probably just a momentary pause, it seemed to go on for a long time. But the school's rector, Dr. Hasan Murad—who would later become a great partner in our work—broke the stillness with a genial call to dinner. I later learned that our antagonist acknowledged he was wrong to challenge me like he did and there was general appreciation for my candor. That was a defining moment in my work with UPIC and with the relationships I have been able to establish with Pakistanis since. I am reminded of how many moments we are called upon to state something that threatens our position, credibility, or power. What we say can alter the course of our entire lives.

I was reminded of my friend Wes Diggs. In December 1975, he was accused of murdering his family—his wife and four children were found executed in their suburban home. Wes was not home when the murders occurred. He was having an affair and at the time he was with the "other woman." During his interrogation by the police on the very night the bodies were discovered, he decided simply to tell the truth and admit to the affair. His objective was to find the killer of his family (forty years later and no one has ever been charged). By risking society's disapproval and remaining faithful to the truth, Wes redirected the investigation away from him and towards other suspects.

I later wrote a book about my friend and described this particular moment in his life thusly:

"Are you having an affair with her?"

It is one of those crossroads in life. Diggs hesitates for a brief instant. He has a decision to make which is crucial. He can tell; he can feel it. Almost without conscious awareness, certainly without verbalizing it, Wesley Diggs realizes that he is a suspect. A suspect: the fact slams into his already beleaguered body like a truck. His family has been brutally molested, to what extent he does not yet even know, and they are accusing him of the awful crime. How could they? The thought cuts like a knife into his very being. The crush of the unspoken accusation tears at him, but his strong sense of survival dictates that *he* must carry on. He knows that whatever has happened to his family is so hideous, so heinous, that all lies must pale before the event. The truth must win out: whatever the cost, whatever the hurdles, he must overcome them. For some fateful reason which he does not fully understand, he must remain a free man. He must find some resolution to their tragedy and his. Absolute truth is his surest defense so he will not lie—not to the police, not to anyone. He decides all this in but the blinking of an eye, in this one brief hesitation, barely perceptible to even the experienced interrogators in the room. He will speak the truth, so that he might be free.

"I have been seeing her, yes."[2]

I have not always been perfect in this pursuit of truth. It was during the sixties and I was in college. The professor wanted to make a point about how the traditional sources of authority were breaking down in our society and so he asked two questions. The first: "How many of you have read *The Catcher in the Rye*? It was a large lecture hall and several hoops and hollers erupted as virtually all two hundred students in attendance put their hands up.

> Remain faithful to the truth, but avoid exaggeration.

"Now," he said, and you knew the zinger was coming, "how many of you have read the Bible?" There was laughter first and then, as I scanned the room, almost no one had their hand up. Not even me. The irony was that I was at that time preparing to go to seminary and so I had read quite a bit of the Bible. But I was embarrassed to say so because for my peers it was a forgone conclusion that it was just not cool to read the Bible anymore. While this was not a moment of particular pride, it did provide a humbling lesson about the courage required to go against the grain, to strike out in opposition to the prevailing social norms. It was an important lesson in my evolving value system—one that would shape my behavior for decades to come.

At the other extreme, it is also important in such moments not to stretch the truth. I recall one incident when I was working for Creative Connections. One of our clients was a local bank and we were producing some promotional material for them. We were asked to do a report that would help them improve their business and we had become aware of some discriminatory practices that were occurring in the way bank personnel treated people of color. I knew of one instance in particular (though I was convinced there were more). I was incensed by this injustice and we mentioned it in our report—it was, frankly, a single line in a report that was perhaps fifty pages long. However, with acute sensitivity to charges of discrimination, at a public session the bank's president zeroed in with laser-like focus on this single line. Now, the bank president was not a particularly nice person. He was known for demeaning staff members and customers alike. He was unaccustomed to being challenged and was angry, to say the least.

"Do you have proof?!" he bellowed.

"Yes," I replied righteously. I did have proof.

"Has it happened more than once?"

"Yes. Multiple times." I did not have proof of this.

"Re-do this report. Include explicit proof of these incidents, with dates, places, and the people involved!"

Since that moment, I have the most profound empathy for every politician or public figure who is suddenly caught in a lie! The untrue words came so easily. I was passionate about what I knew to be true but then immediately panicked that my "exaggeration" would be discovered and I would be held accountable in ways I could not yet imagine. Eventually, nothing of real substance occurred, but these events forever helped me understand how easy it was to stretch the truth, even for the best of reasons. I came away from this experience more wary of my public remarks and more conscious of the need to keep emotions and facts separate.

> Keep emotions and facts separate.

As I was visiting Pakistan in 2012, my family was concerned for my safety and, indeed, not without cause. While we never felt threatened, our hosts had arranged for us to travel with an armed security guard wherever we went, and we were always aware when we were in public places how "different" we were, how little exposure the people of Pakistan have to westerners. Then the week after we left, as if to validate our loved ones' concerns, the Taliban attacked the airport in Peshawar, less than one hundred miles from Islamabad, killing seven people.

But just hours earlier, an unimaginably horrific story was unfolding a world away in Newtown, Connecticut, as a mentally ill Adam Lanza brutally massacred twenty-seven people at close range, twenty of them children ages six or seven. Our hearts clutched and we held our collective breath as we learned about the terror in that elementary school, an incident so incomprehensible that it lies beyond the descriptors words can provide.

A sad, angry, and resolute President Obama told the people of Newtown and all Americans (as he would do almost twenty times throughout his tenure as commander in chief) that "these tragedies must end" and that "I'll use whatever power the office holds" in an effort to prevent future incidents. Sadly, such was not to be the case, as multiple mass shootings took place between the events at Newtown and the end of President Obama's second term.

As the Newtown story unfolded, I couldn't help but wonder how my new Pakistani friends viewed this news. It is one thing to counter the impressions caused by old episodes of *Gilligan's Island* or the great excesses of *American Idol*, but the facts that emerged out of Newtown were true. How were we to reassure our Pakistani counterparts that this is not us? Or is it?

My concern about how Pakistanis and others throughout the world view Americans was rekindled with added vigor during the presidential campaign of 2016. On another visit to Pakistan, this time during the U.S. primary season, I was reminded anew of the way that people from around the world look to our news as evidence of who we are as a global society and where the world is headed. Young people in Pakistan would use a one-word description—Trump—to express alarm over the example the United States was setting and their fear for the future. In all my trips to Pakistan and in all the issues that we discussed at length with community leaders and students, I never experienced the level of anxiety that was expressed during our trip in the spring of 2016, not even five years earlier at the height of the drone strikes on Pakistani soil.

Some months later, an incident in Queens, New York, and its subsequent repercussions again demonstrated the impact that our actions have upon citizens in other lands. On a steamy summer Saturday afternoon, Imam Maulama Akonjee and his associate Thara Uddin were walking home from prayers at the Al-Furqan Jame Masjid dressed in religious garb when they were gunned down execution style. The city's interfaith and community leaders responded with urgency and compassion. The act shocked and horrified New Yorkers, who pride themselves on their embrace of diversity, where anyone can live out their identity peacefully, irrespective of race, religion, national origin, sexual orientation, or gender identity.

While at first the motive was murky, many in the community and beyond blamed the level of hateful rhetoric on the airwaves and in our political discourse as giving tacit license of hate crimes. But there is more. The following month, under the auspices of UPIC, Rabbi Reuven Firestone from Hebrew Union College in Los Angeles and Mr. Ali Tariq from the International Islamic University in Islamabad were to lead American and Pakistani undergraduates in an academic discipline called Scriptural Reasoning, an opportunity to study and discuss ancient sacred texts from both Muslim and Jewish perspectives.

But only hours after the shooting, we received a message from our colleague Ali Tariq, asking to postpone the event. He said, "The [Pakistani students] have started expressing their inability to participate. . . . They are disturbed by yesterday's killing of the Imam and his assistant in New York and say that they cannot participate in any academic/religious activity at this time in these circumstances. Unfortunately this incident has created a great stir and debate in the academic and religious circles here. . . . You can't imagine how disturbed I am after all this . . ."

Violence against American Muslims and hate-filled rhetoric is a combustible mix for Muslims around the world, especially young people, and those who have no firsthand experience in the United States or with Americans. The postponement of a program that seeks to build bridges is but one casualty of this volatile atmosphere. Such a postponement contributes to the cycle of mistrust between our two countries and exposes the height of barriers we must continue to hurdle so that everyone can live in harmony and mutual dignity. The takeaway: More than ever, we must stay the course.

How we respond in the aftermath of such events speaks volumes about who we are as a people. From our personal relationships to our policy reforms, I offer three things I believe we must do: We must cherish our children—let them know that while we cannot always protect them, we will always love them, calm their fears, and nurture their dreams; we must speak openly and courageously about mental illness, removing the stigma of those who suffer from such disorders and work together compassionately towards healing

> Cherish the children; speak openly, courageously and compassionately about mental illness; view gun violence as a public health issue.

and wholeness; and we must view gun violence as a public health issue and enact sensible gun control policies *now*.[3] By so responding, we can become a society that—despite our failures—finds hope in its own resilience and is respected and emulated throughout the world.

In Habakkuk, one of the shortest books in Hebrew Scripture, we find words that I believe to be among the most important lines the Bible has to offer in terms of its implications for Christian theology. They were likely written during the "swirling cauldron" of a collapsing Israel late in the seventh and early sixth centuries BCE.[4] They are relevant to our time because the issues of our day—mass incarceration, climate change, immigration reform, trafficking, ongoing headlines from Iraq and Syria—imply that our society is also a swirling cauldron of collapse.

> O LORD, how long shall I cry for help, and you will not listen? Or cry to you "Violence!" and you will not save? . . . Destruction and violence are before me; strife and contention arise. So the law becomes slack and justice never prevails. The wicked surround the righteous—therefore judgment comes forth perverted. (Hab. 1:2–4)

But remember that God charges us to be instruments of hope, to believe (out loud) in God's grace despite what seems to be all evidence to the contrary. We need look no further than these subsequent, inspiring words from Habakkuk:

> Look at the nations, and see! Be astonished! Be astounded! For a work is being done in your days that you would not believe if you were told. . . . I will stand at my watchpost, and station myself on the rampart; I will keep watch to see what he will say to me, and what he will answer concerning my complaint. Then the LORD answered me and said: Write the vision; make it plain on tablets, so that a runner may read it. For there is still a vision for the appointed time; it speaks of the end, and does not lie. If it seems to tarry, wait for it; it will surely come, it will not delay." (Hab. 1:5–2:3)

And so, this is the response we offer, one that is lived out in the pews of our congregations, in gatherings in Islamabad hosted by Intersections, in the online work of Believe Out Loud and other LGBT justice organizations, among veterans and civilians, political leaders and the 99 percent, among artists and activists, among Christians, Muslims, and Jews in this time and in this place, as we engage in a multifaith affirmation of God's love and justice—a dream that, though not yet realized, is neither impossible nor unattainable, but will never die, and, one day, a dream that will surely come.

15 | Forgiveness

Forgiveness is the fragrance that the violet sheds on the heel that has crushed it.[1]

—*Mark Twain*

One person with whom we have worked with is Azi Hussein, a Pakistani American who has lived in this country most of his life. Several years ago, he met his wife, who had more recently come to this country, fleeing persecution from religious extremists who had terrorized her village and killed her brother.

In part because of this, Azi decided to dedicate his life to interfaith dialogue. He began to work among madrassa leaders in Pakistan in order to counter the fundamentalists who were breeding hatred in some of those schools. While undertaking this work, he also found some brave administrators who were working to modernize the curriculum and promote harmony across cultural and religious divides. Among these administrators was a reformed Taliban commander whose hand would shake uncontrollably. When Azi asked a colleague why his hand shook so violently, he was told that the man was so fearful of Allah's judgment for what he had done in the past—having brutally executed people—that he could not keep his hand still.

Eventually, Azi learned the name of this person. He discovered it was the same man who had killed his brother-in-law years earlier. Azi approached the man face-to-face and told him he forgave him. Humbled by this act, the man asked to speak directly to Azi's wife and, also face-to-face, begged her forgiveness for what he had done to her family. Once again, forgiveness was granted. This man continued to be a powerful voice for redemption in rural Pakistan, his life standing as a witness to what forgiveness can mean.

The prophet Habakkuk asks God, "Why do you neither listen nor act?" Violence is all around us. The law becomes slack and justice never prevails. Oh, God is speaking, alright. But Habakkuk doesn't like the answer, that a heathen king and a heathen army—Nebuchadnezzar and the Babylonians—will discipline his own people. This answer confuses Habakkuk, and he just cannot believe that a pure and holy God would stand idly by and watch them swallow up his people. The prophet is befuddled, impatient. God's response: "Write the vision; make it plain on tablets, so that a runner may read it" (Hab.2:2).

What an amazing passage for us in the frantic world of the twenty-first century. It speaks to the harried executive, the stressed-out pastor, the kid whose schedule has run amuck because of pressure to get into the right college, to the soccer mom who is part-time counselor and full-time chauffeur, to you and to me, because we just can't slow down.

Write the vision. Make it plain. Even in difficult times—in times of budget shortfalls and staff cutbacks, in times of war and threats of new war, in times when society is divided and people are excluded by class and race and age and gender and sexual orientation. Write the vision. Make it plain.

And don't be impatient, but wait for it to be realized in our time. Dr. Cleophus LaRue, an ordained National Baptist and professor of preaching at Princeton Theological Seminary, comments:

> The patience in Habakkuk should be seen as a "wait of anticipation." Habakkuk suggests that this is the way the righteous wait. Their wait is alert and charged with expectation. Their stand is one of tip-toe anticipation. They wait in the fervent hope of a brighter tomorrow morning when night with all its shadows will be passed away.[2]

Trust the vision. This sentiment is replicated in the first chapter of Mark. I love the Gospel of Mark; the writer's economy of language implies a sense of urgency and immediacy. Jesus comes upon some young guys fishing on the Sea of Galilee. He calls out to them, "Follow me" and immediately—"straightaway" in the King James Version—they follow him. No hesitation, no knowledge of the destination. They just follow—immediately . . . straightway.

Listen to these words by David Ewart in *Holy Textures*:

> What is revolutionary about Jesus is not so much his healing, but his hospitality . . . and his radical hospitality which heals social disruptions, is the first step of his healing. . . . If we focus on the **interactions**—the relationships—we see that what is going on is social healing.
>
> Jesus receives everyone: Roman army officer, synagogue leader; tax collector; bleeding woman; leper. People who would otherwise despise each other, avoid being in the same room with each other, are connected because they connect with Jesus. The healing and forgiveness that Jesus provides restores relationships, restores the broken bonds of community.[3]

It is a broad portfolio that we have at Intersections, but the common thread is not in the issues we address as an organization, but in the way we position ourselves at those boundary points, those thin places. We bring people to a common table who would not otherwise be together; and then we provide safe space to listen—often to unexpected or marginalized voices—because it is often through those excluded perspectives that new paradigms emerge. What does this thread hold for us as individuals? Are there "best practices" we can learn from the ways of the world and apply to our individual decision-making?

Back in the 1980s, I left congregational ministry for the "call" to form my own media company, Creative Connections in Media. I was privileged to travel to many parts of the world—literally from the North Slope of Alaska to the townships of South Africa; from the *favelas* of Brazil to rural China—not as a tourist, but as a documentarian of individuals and communities in their struggle for justice and equal opportunity. Rick Reineke, my sound guy, would often say, "Come work for Creative Connections and see the world, one slum at a time!"

But I found honor in telling stories that are often overlooked, amplifying the voices of those who have neither the platform nor any inclination to seek the spotlight but who toil day-in and day-out to make life better for those around them, out of view of media or powerful pundits. Some of those I met left a lasting impression on me.

Decades ago, at the height of the AIDS crisis, we did a story on Yvonne, a beautiful young mother from Brazil infected with AIDS who struggled mightily to care for her young daughter. She was touched by our presence; no one had ever considered her story worthy of being told and now there we were in her small home with the power to tell the world of her courage, her tenderness, and her love for her child.

I remember Anna, the young translator from Armenia, shortly after that country's war with Azerbaijan, who was so proficient in her work and who had a burning dream to come to America. While there, we wrestled with how to tell the story of this country shaking off the communist yoke and trying to right itself in the family of nations. The night before our final day of shooting, I thought—why not make Anna the central storyteller? I asked her if she would consider going "on camera." Her almost nonchalant, one-word response—"sure"—spoke volumes of her willingness to take risks and move beyond her comfort zone.

I later told her that her immediate response, straightaway, had cemented a commitment from me to do all I could to see that she would come to the United States. Eventually, she did as we bent multiple rules with the Immigration and Naturalization Service (INS), and she served as a minimum wage employee with Creative Connections just as we were experiencing financial difficulties. Anna's introduction to this country of great wealth was to be on the front lines of a company as it went through bankruptcy. Yet she went on to have a solid career in media and lives permanently today in the United States.

My time with Creative Connections was filled with poignant moments and often stark visuals. Maybe the single most compelling scene I witnessed occurred in the midst of a massive garbage dump in Brazil. We were there to document the poor communities of garbage pickers who had literally made their homes in the middle of the dump and who scavenged for food and recyclable supplies amidst the trash. I will never forget the excitement of one woman who had located a cake—half of it literally rotten with bugs, but the other half seemingly untouched—as she exuberantly told us that her family would have a sweet treat for supper. We ventured into one of the shacks to do some filming, and the stench was almost unbearable. Yet the folks who lived there were going about their lives as normally as you or I would drive to the grocery store.

Then we captured on video—against a massive landscape of refuse and rot—two boys jubilantly doing cartwheels. The juxtaposition of their playful exuberance against the backdrop of despair was a powerful visual statement about the resilience of the human spirit. It is an image, far beyond what words could capture, forever seared in my consciousness.

16 | 9/11 Ribbons

You don't need hope when things are going well;
you need it when things are not going well.[1]

—*Barack Obama*

In Acts, chapter 10, we meet Cornelius, a Roman army officer. He is not Jewish, but he respects God deeply, gives to charity, and has a robust prayer life. He dreams that he should invite Peter—Jesus' disciple and, of course, a Jew—who is visiting the neighboring town of Joppa, to come to his house. He dreams that he should listen to what Peter has to say.

Meanwhile Peter, too, has been dreaming. He sees a white sheet descending from heaven containing every known animal, clean and unclean. Peter is told to "get up, kill, and eat" but Peter resists. Dietary laws were (and continue to be) a distinct sign of Jewish identity, so to maintain this identity, he refuses. But a voice in Peter's dream declares, "What God has made clean, you shall not call unclean" (Acts 10:15).

Just then, messengers arrive from Cornelius, and Peter greets them, invites them to spend the night, and then goes with the men to Caesarea, where Cornelius lives. Peter is not sure where he's going or what he is to do; he is only sure that God is directing him. When Peter arrives at Cornelius' house, the two men talk openly, sharing their dreams. And then Peter preaches a sermon, beginning with the words: "I now know that God knows no partiality" (Acts 10:34). It was a startling declaration then, and for many of us who become rooted into calcified identities—religious, ethnic, ideological—it may be just as startling today. How easy it is to assume that God's Word can come to us only through traditional sources and in customary ways.

Then, according to Scripture, the Holy Spirit came upon Cornelius and his family, showing everyone that these Gentiles were full members of the family of faith. Peter asks the question that was relevant in the moment, but is equally important for us today, set in a broader context: "Can anyone withhold the water for baptizing these people?" (Acts 10:47).

In this instance, Peter is very concrete in his use of the word "water," but the symbolic message is much wider. Can anyone withhold the water? When God is in our midst, is there any power that can really stop the flood of God's justice for overcoming humanity's prejudice, fear, inhospitality, violence, and greed? We might not fully understand the timing, we might get discouraged by setbacks along the way, but, really—can anything stop the "rain" of God's mercy? God is so vast and our attempts to limit God's activity in history so filled with folly and an inflated sense of power, can anyone stop the rain?

In New York City—and well beyond—there was a raging debate over building a Muslim community center in lower Manhattan near the site of the twin towers. The "ground zero mosque" controversy achieved international notoriety. I attended the Landmarks Commission meeting where those who opposed this center used the argument that the building at 47–51 Park Place should not be converted to a Muslim community center because part of the plane that flew into the World Trade Center on 9/11 had fallen onto its roof; hence it should be made a landmark building.

An elder in the Collegiate Church, Christopher Moore, who also served for a time as chair of the Intersections Board of Directors, is a noted historian and a member of the city's Landmarks Preservation Commission. He rose to speak to this controversy. His concluding words: "Whether the cast iron rusts and falls apart, or whether it is replaced by the most famous community center in the world, or a church, its space will always memorialize the people who were in those planes, and in those buildings, and in the sky. Last I looked, we do not landmark the sky . . . I do not support the designation.[2]

> Can anyone withhold the water?
> Can anyone landmark the sky?

Chris's role on the Commission and his remarks that day were pivotal in the crisis engulfing our city—and the whole world. They echoed Peter's words so many centuries before. The contexts were radically different, but the content was the same: Who can hold back the water? Who can landmark the sky? These are God's realm and we, if we are to be faithful, must be stewards of history and not resistant to God's work in the world.

So, our question then becomes "how" do we sing a new song? How do we turn the tide of violence and hatred in our midst? What is the language of our lyrics, the rhyme and meter of our verses? What is the imagery we use in our choruses? What are the instruments we play to create this new song?

Like everyone else in the United States born before the turn of the twenty-first century, I have my 9/11 story. The anniversary of that fateful date prompts each of us to recall where we were when we heard the news, how we reacted, what we thought about our loved ones who were further away than arm's reach, how we envisioned the future. Especially if you lived in New York, the anniversary evokes powerful memories as we connect our very personal experiences to what—even in its earliest moments—was clearly an event that would forever change our world.

I was not in New York, but was serving as director of communication at the United Church of Christ's national offices in Cleveland. I was at a staff meeting when I heard the news. Like the Kennedy assassination forty years earlier, you can remember exactly where you were when you first heard that towers were struck. Our communications staff literally sprang into motion and within the hour we had a story on the home page of the UCC's website. Fifteen years ago, this was an incredibly fast turnaround. As a result, many people turned to our site for updates (we were online earlier than some major news services), establishing a viewing habit that kept them tuned in for weeks. Even that first day, we updated the story frequently, trying to separate fact from rumor, sharing news about the attack on the Pentagon, Shanksville, President Bush's response, pervasive fears from elected officials and ordinary citizens alike.

Downtown Cleveland was evacuated. My daughter Kierra was living in Greenwich Village at the time, just blocks from the twin towers. Phone lines were jammed. I couldn't reach her for hours. I needed to stay on the job, and I recall the agonizing tug between checking on her welfare and doing the work I felt called to do. There was no reason for her to be at the World Trade Center, but still—it was only a few blocks away and a father's worry is not always dictated by logic.

Kristin and her husband were traveling in Canada and were expected to return home that very day. In fact, they crossed the border just before it was closed. Blythe was babysitting our four-year-old grandson, Chase. I could not reach them either, but we were hundreds of miles from New York or Washington and any danger seemed remote. (I later learned that Flight 93—the fourth hijacked aircraft—turned around over Cleveland. By that time all aircraft were grounded, but Blythe reported having seen a plane make a sharp turn high overhead—a scary thought.) With Chase focused on various blocks and stuffed animals on the living room floor, the TV continued to broadcast in the background, scenes of the carnage in downtown Manhattan replaying over and over again.

Late in the afternoon, as Cleveland implemented its evacuation plans and we retired the website for the evening, I returned home to the palpable relief of wife and grandson. His parents were close to Cleveland and we decided to meet them for dinner at our favorite Middle Eastern restaurant nearby (the irony of that decision was lost on us until later that night!). By that time we had also contacted Kierra in the Village, who, though she was physically unharmed, was emotionally spent and scarred by seeing the second tower fall from her rooftop vantage point just a few blocks away.

But the truly memorable image for me—at the intersection of memory and imagination—occurred a bit later in the evening. We lived on the top floor of a condo on Lake Erie. Our elevator had a window through which its passengers could see the Cleveland skyline in the distance. I will never forget Chase's childlike glee as he spied the skyline—he was too young to realize *which* skyline—and exclaimed with unimaginable glee, "New York City!" In his young mind, after living through hours of background noise filled with the twin towers falling again and again, the sight of a skyline standing peacefully against the gathering darkness released in him a most profound shriek of joy and relief—and hope for the future. He told me recently that the view of that skyline evoked in him feelings of joy and wonder within a context of what he sensed, even before his fourth birthday, was "a worried vibe" that filled his family and the wider world on that day.

Almost a decade later, that "worried vibe" had turned into an atmosphere of hostility, acrimony, and the threat of violence in New York City in the wake of an angry controversy over creating a Muslim community center in lower Manhattan near the site of the World Trade Center terrorist attack in 2001. What was revealed in the often vitriolic and hostile debate about the so-called "Ground Zero Mosque" in New York City during the summer of 2010 was that this was the "conversation we never had" post–9/11.

The debate was sparked by ongoing suspicion of Islam and the Muslim community on the part of some New Yorkers, and then fueled by politicians and pundits who used fear-mongering and demonizing to promote an intolerant and hate-filled agenda that drove a wedge between communities and neighborhoods. Imam Feisal Abdul Rauf was a lightning rod for these attacks. His concept of a Muslim community center that would serve all

New Yorkers was vilified as a subversive mega-mosque that would destroy American values and enslave our people.

There was genuine fear that violence would erupt, especially as the city approached the ninth anniversary of 9/11. While managing to avoid violence then, many imagined a much different fate for the tenth anniversary. It would be, many feared, an occasion that could inflame the embers of bigotry and fear that lay just below the surface in so many places. The voice of concerned religious leaders seemed largely absent from the public debate; spiritual values of harmony and tolerance were muted.

And so six multifaith organizations from around the city began to meet to avoid such a possibility as the tenth anniversary of that tragedy approached. The name of our coalition: Prepare New York. Our purpose: To equip New Yorkers and others to engage across lines of faith, culture, neighborhood, and political perspective in order to make what our U.S. Constitution calls a "more perfect union." We developed a multipronged strategy in the hope that other communities who face trauma or who encounter division might learn from us and employ some of the techniques we used.

The six initial organizations grew to a network of more than one hundred companies, congregations, and organizations, ranging from the Roman Catholic Archdiocese of New York, with its four hundred congregations and 2.6 million members, to the Jain Association of North America.

In recognizing that the mainstream media in the United States was a principle agent in promoting the hate-filled rhetoric that surrounded the so-called Ground Zero Mosque, we created media resources to counter that narrative and a social networking strategy to spread the message of reconciliation and peace. We produced a video, *We The People*, that showed the long history of religious tolerance *and* intolerance in America.[3] Our hope was that such a historical context—including prejudice against Catholics and Quakers, Jews and Japanese, who have now become part of the mainstream—would give us hope that intolerance towards Muslims, so virulent in the early years of the twenty-first century—would also pass, if Americans would work towards that more perfect union.

Religious leaders underwent media training: We produced an online curriculum on religious tolerance for use in classrooms, congregations, workplaces, and private homes that offered conceptual reasons for intolerance and practical means of building bridges across lines of difference. "Coffee Hour Conversations" were held across the city whereby individuals had an opportunity to approach one another, get to know each other's story, learn about one another's faith and culture, and begin to build the personal relationships essential to community trust and harmony.

And, on the weekend of September 11, we held two events that offered an opportunity for people to participate in acts of healing. The first was a traditional Buddhist Lantern Ceremony in which thoughts or prayers in memory of those who were lost are collected and placed in paper lanterns. The lanterns were then floated on the Hudson River in the shadow of where the twin towers once stood—creating a moving visual image. Religious leaders from far beyond the Abrahamic traditions led prayers.

The second was our Ribbons of Hope event, directed by our son-in-law, Joe Parlagreco. In this project we found a simple—this is key—activity that people could do to take part in an expression of healing. We invited people to write down on a ribbon their thought or prayer or hope for the healing of the world. We then asked people to bring their ribbons to lower Manhattan where they would attach them to twelve nine-foot-tall panels that created tapestries of different colors and textures and shapes and sizes—symbolic of the rich diversity that is found in the human condition.

Journeying down to lower Manhattan in an atmosphere of memory of the past and imagination for a better world reversed the flight of fear and suspicion that so many New Yorkers took a decade earlier, replacing it with a path that looked forward to a world of peace. Before we were finished, more than thirty thousand had participated—9/11 survivors and children who were not yet born on the day of the attacks; farmers from Missouri and college students from California; senior citizens from Pennsylvania's Amish country and third graders from Budapest; Catholic priests and Buddhist monks; short ribbons and long ribbons, in different colors, textures, shapes, and sizes, each carrying its own distinctive message and, when taken together, an outpouring of hope and healing, reflective of our magnificent human diversity.

It was humbling to hear the stories of remembrance from those who came by, and inspirational to see the messages of hope for the future. Kevin Jones, a local musician, contributed a piece of music, "Shadows," he had written shortly after the attack on the World Trade Center, and my friend Cliff Aerie put a series of still photos to the music.[4] Audiences as far away as Central Asia were touched by our multifaith efforts to ensure the peace across the city.

The twelve tapestry panels were then displayed throughout the city, part of a year-long plan to bring them to different locations—secular and religious—as an ongoing, expanding, interactive witness for peace. The first batch of more than one thousand ribbons to come to Intersections after the 9/11 weekend anniversary included some from Israel. The ribbons were from Israeli Arabs and Jews, with some from the West Bank. They were written in Arabic, Hebrew, and English.

As I was hanging these expressions of peace, I happened to place these multilingual messages next to a bright yellow ribbon that proclaimed, "ensemble toujours," which my rudimentary French translated as "always together." How fitting. During the Christmas season, the ribbons were on display at the Cathedral of St. John the Divine on Manhattan's Upper West Side, including the time that the Paul Winter Consort played its annual Winter Solstice Concert. Mayor Michael Bloomberg paid tribute to this project at his annual New Year's Eve Interfaith Breakfast at the New York Public Library.

The key principles in this process resonate as we seek to create and implement concrete, constructive projects that can heal the world: (1) grow your base and be intentional about diversity; (2) share authoritative knowledge to combat those who would offer simplistic and often inaccurate answers to current controversies; (3) engage the media—they are a powerful force—understand the pressures on them, but prepare well so that you can articulate your message of peace and reconciliation; (4) provide an easy, accessible way that large numbers of people can participate—including children; and (5), finally, develop an ongoing vehicle that keeps your message alive and vibrant so that you can continue to transform lives and communities.

Oh, and one final thing—in New York on the tenth anniversary of September 11, despite a "terrorist alert" that came from Washington, there was no violence. Those who tried to spew hate held some rallies, but almost no one attended and there was virtually no media coverage. And, in perhaps the most significant symbol of the success of that weekend, when the authorities searched the truck—which they did frequently—as we moved staging equipment for our weekend events into lower Manhattan, they went looking for bombs, but found only ribbons.

> They went looking for bombs, but found only ribbons.

Fast forward three years, and more memories—just as vivid, but now including an underlying serenity—perhaps it was a society finally coming to grips with its most tragic day. It was just before sunset at the 9/11 Memorial. The day was incredibly beautiful—bright, warm, dry—one of those days that happen all too infrequently in New York City. It was 2014, and I had just walked the streets of lower Manhattan in a 9/11 "Unity Walk" commemorating that horrific day. That evening, we seemed on the brink of yet another military intervention in the Middle East, heightening the emotional context for our walk and our gathering at the memorial.

We began at St. Andrew's Roman Catholic Church and stopped for refreshments and remarks at Masjid Manhattan, then gathered as the sun was sinking low—what those in the film industry call "the golden hour"—for a prayer service at the 9/11 Memorial. The widely diverse gathering drew in close to hear thoughts and prayers from Buddhist, Christian, and Zoroastrian clergy. I was reminded again about the richness of our diversity in this city and across the planet, and how that is a gift we so easily take for granted.

What followed was one of those magical moments that transcend time and space, sight and sound. The 9/11 Memorial is a spacious place, park-like in its setting. The late afternoon sun filtered through the trees, creating dappled patterns all around. The area is dominated by two immense water sculptures that descend below ground and mark the footprint where the towers once stood. An expansive stillness settled over the landscape.

And then, from the center of our interfaith prayer circle, the resonant tones of opera singer Tomoko Shibata concluded our time together with the deeply familiar words to "Amazing Grace." You could sense how this unexpected melody impacted those who simply happened to be present at the memorial on that late Sunday afternoon—the time and place sharpening the senses, the sound of singing mingling with the cascading waterfalls and the humming city in the background. This beloved song—"amazing grace, how sweet the sound"—was an ode to remembrance, transcendent words of hope for a more peaceful tomorrow.

Forces far beyond the control of those few souls who were gathered with us seemed to have—at least momentarily—halted the relentless march to further violence. Millions offered prayers and songs for peace that weekend, among them our small gathering with its golden moment, when many hearts joined a single voice. As they say, when a single butterfly flaps its wings . . . So, who is to say that our prayers and that song—along with the songs and prayers for peace from so many millions more—may not have provided the tipping point to turn us aside from war.

Will lives be changed generations from now because of these reflections, uplifted by the dappled sunshine, the wafting of musical notes in the afternoon stillness, the special moment on that special anniversary? Only time will tell. Will some of those present be affected in the same way I was by Phil Sheridan or my high school coach Don Frisina or my visits with Eurika Freema or my relationship with Wes Diggs? Will they

A simple action can launch events that change the course of history.

be prompted to make transformational changes so that their lives are altered and history shifts? We cannot be sure.

But the point is, we never know how a seemingly simple act of kindness or courage can begin a series of events—a butterfly flapping her wings— that shifts the course of history. Therefore, we must be constant and diligent in how we relate to one another and to the created universe that surrounds us. And when our capacities diminish, we need to shift our own expectations, knowing that the impressions we leave can still be profound and lasting, long beyond our lifetimes.

17 | Ancestors

Old men ought to be explorers
Here and there does not matter
We must be still and still moving
Into another intensity . . .
In my end is my beginning.[1]

—*T. S. Eliot*

One of my earliest memories is of a vacation in New Hampshire. I was three. Vacations were a real treat in my youth. We only had two weeks and it was the only time we traveled. New Hampshire, with its mountain ranges and lush vegetation seemed a world away from the paved streets and parking lots of Long Island, where I grew up.

One day, my father and I went for a hike up the mountainside through the deep woods. I recall that, although the day was bright, the canopy of the forest made it seem like dusk. It was awesome for a three-year-old whose only association with woods was the undeveloped scrub beneath the power lines in our Levittown neighborhood. And, while this was probably my imagination, it seemed that the further we went, the darker and scarier it became.

We rounded a bend to see a clearing ahead. Suddenly, standing majestically in the glinting sun, was a ram—perhaps the first wild animal I had ever seen. He seemed huge to my three-year-old senses, imposing as he stared at the intruders in his sunlit realm. I was overwhelmed by the raw power and energy and freedom that I witnessed. For me, all these years later, it remains a startling reminder of the wonder and grandeur of the natural world.

> Be amazed. Be astounded. Creation is abundant and filled with miracles, if we but take the time to notice.

The International Union for Conservation of Nature's Red List claims that more than twelve thousand species (out of forty thousand assessed) face some extinction risk, including one bird in eight, 13 percent of the world's flowering plants, and a quarter of all mammals.[2] A global study published in *Nature* that took ten years to complete concluded that 21 percent of all fish species are deemed "at risk."[3] An Antarctic ice bridge, holding a vast ice shelf in place, shattered in pieces, one of ten ice shelves that have shrunk or collapsed because of the past fifty years of warming.[4] In the Arctic, thinner seasonal ice now makes up 70 percent of the winter ice, up from 40 percent in the 1980s. Scientists fear that Arctic seas will be entirely ice free in the summer months by 2045.[5] The signs abound as to the fragility of our world. How can we be faithful in the midst of the environmental devastation that surrounds us?

Many ecologists and others have argued that the command to humanity in Genesis 1:26 defines the crisis we face.[6] For example, historian Lynn White Jr. claims that the relationship between humankind and the world, which has resulted in the continuing destruction of nature, has come about because of "the orthodox Christian arrogance towards nature, following the imperative of the Genesis command."[7] White blames our Western attitude of earth exploitation on that part of the Judeo-Christian tradition that conceives of human beings as superior to all the rest of creation, which was formed simply for our use.

So what do we do? My practice, when confronted with unanswerable questions has been to turn to the Bible for guidance. But what do you do when the text itself is problematic, as in the Genesis passage? You return again to the text itself, dig deeper, and seek greater enlightenment. When I did this, I discovered the counterbalance to both dominionism and the false promise of technological nirvana in words from the book of Job:

> [7]"But ask the animals, and they will teach you; the birds of the air, and they will tell you; [8]ask the plants of the earth, and they will teach you; and the fish of the sea will declare to you. [9]Who among all these does not know that the hand of the LORD has done this? [10]In his hand is the life of every living thing and the breath of every human being." (Job 12:7–10)

We cannot let the understanding of our relationship to the planet begin and end in a single verse from Genesis, or even in the history and tradition of the church. If we do, we unleash the devastating power of proof texting, a practice that has brought pain and suffering to generations of believers and has kept countless potential believers at bay because they get "stuck" on a single verse or image. Ask generations of women who have struggled against patriarchy. Ask people of color how the defense of slavery rooted in the Bible brought incarceration, violence, and systemic racism. Ask gay, lesbian, bisexual, and transgender persons how a handful of texts have wrought all kinds of license for destructive behavior towards them in the name of religion.

The image that has lingered for me for half a century has been that of the powerful ram poised in the pool of sunlight against the darkened verdant forest. We are all just stewards of the earth, mindful of its grandeur and intricate diversity. We do not own the moon and the sky. It is ours to cherish and protect. Nowhere is this more true than our responsibility toward the people of the earth.

In high school I read William Golding's *The Inheritors*. The book tells the story of one of the last remaining tribes of Neanderthals at the hands of the more sophisticated homo sapiens. One by one, the adults among the Neanderthals die off or are killed. The children are kidnapped by the "new people." The book is a sad and—because it is rooted in the experience of a single band of this ancient species—intimate account of what it must be like to be the last one left of one's species. These insights and images have become increasingly relevant in our twenty-first-century world where our short-sightedness has caused so much chaos in creation.[8]

In a well-known Native American tale, a wise grandmother took her grandson to the crest of a cliff and there in a cloud formation were two wolves, faced off against each other. "Look carefully," the grandmother said, "and you'll see that one wolf is filled with anger and greed, with bigotry and violence. Look again, and you will see the other is filled with wonder and hope, humility and grace." The grandmother became silent, as if awaiting an epic battle in the sky. "Which one wins?" asked the grandson. "The one you feed, my child, the one you feed."

In 2009, on the four hundredth anniversary of Henry Hudson entering into what would ultimately become New York harbor, there was considerable hoopla surrounding "all things Dutch." The leadership of the Collegiate Church, with Dutch antecedents, felt this was insufficient—bordering on unjust—as there was no comparable recognition of those who were already here when Hudson sailed up the harbor—the Lenape people.

In response, the Collegiate Church, in an unprecedented move, acknowledged their complicity in imposing an alien social, legal, and economic structure on the Lenape people, by writing a statement seeking forgiveness into their official minutes. The leadership of the church then reached out to the Lenape people to hold a day of atonement in lower Manhattan, which was attended by hundreds and which marked the beginning of a new era in the relationship between these two communities.

Committing to a sustained relationship, the Collegiate Church joined with members of the Lenape community to forge a new way of working together to lift the profile of Native American voices in New York City. Both Collegiate and the Lenape were intentional about structuring a relationship that would not last just for a day, but would reach far into the future—extending even for seven generations.

On November 27, 2009, the Collegiate Church of New York observed the first national Native American Heritage Day (as designated by President Obama in June)[9] with Healing Turtle Island: An Event of Cultural Reconciliation between the Collegiate Church and the Lenape people. "Turtle Island" is a reference among Native American people for the land that European settlers called "the new world." This event marked a moment of reconciliation between the two groups, with the Collegiate Church publicly apologizing for the actions of its forbearers during the purchase, and for imposing a different economic system on the Lenape people that caused hardship, violence, and death. The church was the "company church" of the Dutch West Indies Company that "purchased" Manahatta (now Manhattan) from the local Native American tribe.

The event was covered by more than 350 news outlets across the country and another couple dozen overseas. Those news stories could not capture the sense of acknowledgement, acceptance, forgiveness, and resolve to move forward in a new way that was present in downtown Manhattan that blustery day after Thanksgiving. And, perhaps, even more important developments were afoot—far beyond the emotions that overflowed in the park.

Rabbi Marc Gopin, from George Mason University's Institute for Conflict Analysis and Resolution and a seasoned conflict resolution expert on a global scale, told me that our event's rootedness in specific historic events is precisely what gives it both its power and its global relevance. "Invaders," Gopin said, "become disconnected from the lands they invade. This disconnection is partly responsible for our current global ecological crisis. Only when outsiders acknowledge their role as conquerors, can healing happen between peoples and even in the land itself." Indeed, I hoped the collaborative process we used in producing Healing Turtle Island could serve as a model for reconciliation in other settings where unjust structures have been imposed upon indigenous people.

One remarkable aspect of Healing Turtle Island was how many Lenape told me that in addition to a time for healing between Native Americans and those of European ancestry, they also found the day to be a moment of reconciliation among their own people. Curtis Zunigha, former chief of the Delaware (Lenape) Tribe of Indians in Oklahoma spoke in a press conference after the event about how privileged he was to meet leaders of other Lenape bands for the first time. One social media activist told me, "I really believe this was a positive watershed moment. I am highly optimistic; this is a new day for healing. I have never seen such warm smiles on the faces of my Native American friends before. They were truly happy."

Fast forward five years. In the fall of 2014, the concert opera *Purchase of Manhattan* became the latest and most ambitious of these healing projects, an important element in our unfolding partnership. The opera, which tells the story of that historic purchase through the eyes of Native Americans, premiered a week before Thanksgiving, with almost six hundred attending.

"It's showing a new way of being, a new way of projecting of how people can live together by acknowledging past sins . . . to create something new and fresh," I said at the time. "Throughout the past five years, the Lenape and their kin have been witness to the enduring commitment made five years ago as the Collegiate Church, open to exposing this old wound, has been dedicated in concrete ways to a new spirit of cooperation founded on mutual respect and affection. It takes the myth of the 'purchase for $24 worth of beads and trinkets' from a Native American perspective. Presenting the opera at Marble Collegiate Church—the very heart of power in colonial efforts to control the environment and its indigenous inhabitants—sends a powerful message. This 'intersection' is an important step in healing."[10]

The Lenape Center's executive director, Joe Baker, said he recognized an important role the opera could play in promoting and perpetuating Lenape culture through the arts. He called the opera a homecoming. "We really are retelling the early beginnings of New York City."[11] Inspiration for the opera came from Mohican writer and composer Brent Michael Davids, who described the performance as an "opera with movie score sensibility and rich orchestral sound," and a mix between a Broadway performance and opera.

"We're still here."

There are no costume or set changes, and the opera is told in English, with accents of Native American melodies and singing. "Native American culture is still not understood," Davids said. "The stereotype is, the real Indians lived years ago, not now. So we're still invisible. We're still here, but we're rendered invisible. The opera is designed to make people aware of who we are."[12]

Joe Baker added in the *Huffington Post*, "I feel strongly that the appropriate platform for the telling of this complicated and at times conflicted history [of the Lenape people] is the arts. . . . When we had the opportunity to work with Brent Michael Davids to create an original work that spoke to this moment in history . . . we felt that we were fulfilling our mission."[13]

Baker said he hoped the performance would have a "redemptive quality" that would help the now widely dispersed Lenape people chart a course for the future. He emphasized that many people wrongly interpret Native American culture as being a frozen in time, but that it continues growing and evolving. "By embracing contemporary forms of art we can realize and express our true selves and our culture," Baker said. "I hope [the opera] inspires others to join with us in this effort to begin to celebrate our diverse histories within the city in new ways."[14]

"There has been such a void through the centuries due to the history that once occurred here that we want to support initiatives and programs that allow for people themselves to tell their stories," said Hadrien

Coumans, co-founder and director of Lenape Center. He is hopeful that these initiatives will expand beyond New York City, even internationally. He sees the city as a unique opportunity for the Lenape presence to expand because "the cultural values that are Lenape I think are very important with the current state of affairs in the world regarding conflict, climate change. These are all of the areas that we really need to come together and work on, and heal from."[15]

18 | Balance

Can you imagine us years from today,
Sharing a park bench quietly?
How terribly strange to be seventy.[1]

—Paul Simon

remember the first time I heard Simon and Garfunkel's album *Bookends*. I was in college, sprawled out with my girlfriend on the living room rug in her parents' Long Island home. The world seemed a place of infinite possibilities. Paul Simon's storytelling coupled with Art Garfunkel's harmonies touched a place in my soul that few singers had ever reached. So, in this my inaugural hearing, my senses were keen to both lyrics and melodies as I placed myself in the settings the songs illuminated. And when we came to the mournful "Old Friends," it was with quaint romanticism that I listened, trying to imagine myself on that park bench. Ahh, but that seemed so very, very far in the future. There was so much to see, so much to do.

As I move deeper into my later years, I look for the eternal in the momentary. During a relentless period of inclement weather in 2015, I was heading home from a doctor's appointment and then to a sleepover weekend with grandkids Sonoma and Nico. I never made it. It seems that I slipped on some black ice caused by a drizzle that immediately froze onto very cold asphalt surfaces. I awoke about three hours later in our local ER with no memory of how I got there. I had badly bruised ribs, a sprained wrist, facial lacerations that took ten stitches to close, a severe concussion, bleeding on the brain, and memory loss.

It took my wife three hours to locate me. I spent additional days in intensive care before, once my head gradually cleared and the bleeding ceased, I was released from the hospital. Although I still had no recollection of my fall, I seemed to be returning to normal in good stead—or so I thought—and was back at work full time within a couple weeks.

Something had changed. My cognitive powers had suffered in ways I found difficult to identify or describe. I had trouble "connecting the dots," or making stories in my head that had a logical chronology. I couldn't figure out how to approach simple tasks like putting away holiday decorations.

At first, I didn't speak about this at all. It wasn't that I was unable to articulate my new reality; rather, I was afraid to express out loud what I knew to be different. I had changed and I had no way to measure that change; no previous life experience was quite like it. Self-doubt and feelings of uncertainty became overwhelming. How long would this last? Would I fully recover? Would I again be able to formulate memories, images, projections for the future that are essential to my work and a very important part of my psyche? Would my job be in jeopardy? Should I stay quiet, cover my shortcomings in excuses and hope things would return to the way they had been? Could I lower my expectations just enough so people wouldn't notice?

For several years, Intersections' Veteran Civilian Dialogue (VCD) program had been one of Intersections' primary priorities. I had been in countless conversations with veterans, some of whom had returned home with post-traumatic stress or traumatic brain injury, memory loss, and stories of fears, losses, and grief seemingly too painful to retell. I had been awed by the courage of these returning service personnel who were willing to share their stories, sometimes with complete strangers—and who had listened attentively to the stories of civilians like me, stories that seemed to pale in comparison.

My fall was in a very safe zone (on my own street, as it turns out). There was no combat, no fear of IEDs or snipers. The "enemy" was (apparently) a simple patch of black ice. Yet this incident led me to understand at a deeper level than ever before how terrifying it is to wonder if you will re-bound from a trauma, if you will ever recapture who you were before your "life changed," if you will be able to do what you love with the same vigor, if you will watch your grandchildren grow. Yes, I thought about these things *a lot*, especially early on.

And so, swallowing my pride at the seemingly innocuous event that shook me so profoundly, and taking my cues from those with whom I had been in conversation, I began to speak about this incident with a new sense of urgency, seeing it as my duty both personally and professionally.

Soon after, I read Phil Klay's op ed in *The New York Times*. A four-year Marine who served in Iraq and a graduate of Dartmouth and Hunter College, Klay posits an essential truth for the healing of our society from the impact of war on us all. His position is that veterans need to hear from civilians and that civilians should not be led to believe that their voices are irrelevant, that their stories are not valid. Says Klay, "We pay political consequences when civilians are excused or excluded from discussion of war. . . . The notion that the veteran is the unassailable authority on the experience of war shuts down conversation. . . . If we fetishize trauma as incommunicable, then

> We pay political consequences when civilians are excused and excluded from discussion of war.

survivors are trapped—unable to feel truly known by their nonmilitary friends and family. . . . You don't honor someone by telling them, 'I can never imagine what you've been through.' Instead, listen to their story and try to imagine being in it, no matter how hard and uncomfortable that feels."[2]

I am not a veteran, but my experience opened my understanding of the role that trauma can play—often when we least expect it—at a more profound level than before. I had also learned that silence does not serve us well. Strengthened by those I met in our VCD program, I decided to share my own experience widely, willing to risk questioning gazes and wondering minds (Is he really who he was? Is he suffering from a relapse?) in the hope that my rather safe, civilized "trauma" could open a window for us—civilian and veteran alike—on the need to share the truth of our experience. We all need to be open to one another's stories if we are truly to heal from the trauma of war and its impact on us all.

Sometime thereafter, I wrote about this experience in my weekly Intersections blog. It seems I had touched a chord, as the blog received more response—by far—than anything I had written before or since. I found one response particularly moving in its honesty. It was from Christina Andersen. Tina worked with my friend and musical legend, Paul Winter, but her communication with me was about her own experience recovering from a stroke, which was deeply personal. We featured her words on our blog as a way of being in solidarity with countless others who experience unanticipated life-altering realities that are difficult to share. The lesson for both Tina and me: Share these stories, knowing you are not alone.[3]

Two years would pass before I addressed this loss of cognitive capacity publicly. It was in a sermon at Union Congregational UCC in Montclair, New Jersey. Once again, it was motivated by realizations that became all too apparent during a couple of Sunday services.

I have a really good friend—the former director of the Stony Point Conference Center, Rev. Bill Pindar. About thirty years ago, Bill, who is one of the most creative people I have ever met, taught me how to connect the dots on seemingly unrelated elements in order to create a new whole. One of the techniques Bill used to get people thinking about the relationship between the real world and the spiritual realm was an exercise using peacock feathers.

The only way to "balance" the feather on the edge of your finger is to "focus and be flexible," watching the "eye" of the feather and being flexible as the winds buffet it about. If we want our church to be transformative," I preached, "we need to be focused and flexible, both resolute in our commitment to Christ's call for justice and radical hospitality, and nimble enough to respond to the unexpected winds of God's unfolding history in our midst."

Focus and be flexible.

I then shared with the congregants the question that had been occupying my consciousness for weeks: What happens when your life circumstances cause you to lose your flexibility? I recounted how, for years, I was in robust health, played three sports in high school and basketball in college for a top-ten division-one team; how in my work, I was known to keep ridiculously intense schedules and quickly move from one commitment to the next; how all-nighters were routine, and how my video crew would make fun of me, repeating over and over behind my back, "gotta go; gotta go" because of the way I would drive them while on location.

I recounted how a succession of incidents shifted my reality: a shoulder replacement, the severe concussion, a hip replacement, cardio issues, and, just a few weeks prior to my sermon, the sudden dislocation of the same hip that had been replaced seven months earlier. These events conspired against me, leaving me more limited, more inflexible, and prompted me to wonder about what this means about my life, my work, my faith. I am not who I used to be. How does this change my relationship to myself? To my family? To my community? To my God? I marveled about my dad who, at ninety-three, was still engaged in life, although slowed considerably, but who was able to maintain his dignity while living in a time of diminished capacity. I wondered if, as I aged, I would be able to maintain such dignity.

In the midst of the sermon preparation, something else happened. In an activity on "Homecoming Sunday," members of the congregation were asked to create panels out of verses from the first chapter of Genesis. On the front lawn of the church, my wife, Blythe, and I selected verse 3: "Then God said, 'Let there be light'; and there was light." And I made a scene from nature—sunlight and clouds on the flowers—not theologically correct, as the dry land didn't come until later, but pretty enough. Except . . . I made the three backwards!

Only when we came into the sanctuary and saw the other threes did I realize that mine was . . . *backwards*. How many times have I written a three in my life? Yet I had lost the ability to recognize the correct placement of lines in that very familiar numeral. The lingering cognitive disability caused by my concussion led me to create a backwards three—and I didn't even realize it. At that moment, I knew that not only had my flexibility become impaired, but so had my ability to focus. What did this mean? Oh, sure. I could easily laugh this off and say it doesn't matter. I was probably preoccupied or distracted by some seemingly important concern. But it *does* matter. My brain was different than it had been. What did this mean about who I am?

There is more to the story. When we came to worship the following week, my three was turned around by some well-meaning soul, but if you looked carefully, you'd see the flowers were on top and the clouds were below. It was not *my* three, but reconstructed to "fit in" with the others. The well-intentioned church had tried to put my work in a box that didn't deviate from the norm. But actually, I liked my three the way it was—upside down and backwards. It was distinctively mine and that meant something important to me.

> Affirm differences, even if they are upside down and backwards.

This experience prompted me to ask the rhetorical question about those in the human family who never have the ability to be flexible or to focus. What is their relationship to the communities that surround them? What is our relationship to them? Are we to turn their threes over so as to make them fit in? Or are we to celebrate the backwards threes in our midst?

19 | Beyond Death

If there is a scheme,

perhaps this too is in the scheme,

as when a subway car turns on a switch,

the wheels screeching against the rails,

and the lights go out—

but are on again in a moment.[1]

—Charles Reznikoff

At the very beginning of my tenure at Intersections, I knew that if we were to be successful, there were three "givens." First, we had to be prepared to fail. In undertaking something so totally new, if we did not give ourselves the freedom to fail, then we had not taken any risks. Second, we needed to be prepared for controversy. If we were to really make a difference in the world, controversy was inevitable. Third, we needed to "let go." If we were to be serious about addressing the conflicting issues of our day, we must develop decision-making processes that were expansive and invited broad participation. If we sought a world-class operation, we needed to build partnerships that extended beyond our own circles and into unimagined ways that God would lead us.

> Be prepared to fail,
> expect controversy,
> know when to let go.

There is a story I often tell about the "true" founding of Intersections: This ministry actually began on June 25, 1891, in Long Branch, New Jersey. On that night, twenty-three-year-old Frederick Brokaw, son of the fabulously wealthy Fifth Avenue clothier Isaac Brokaw, drowned while trying to save the life of Annie Doyle, a young Irish servant girl.

Frederick's grieving parents, in honor of the heroic act of their son, gave properties called the Bethany Memorial Buildings to Madison Avenue Reformed Church. Ownership of this campus was subsequently transferred to the Collegiate Church and the sale of this property is what has made Intersections possible.

So, it was—at its beginnings—a ministry of intersections: where this heir from New York City's Fifth Ave. made the ultimate sacrifice for the then discounted Irish servant girl from Long Branch, New Jersey. More than a hundred years later, we had the opportunity to continue this heroic legacy in amazing ways. In honor of both Frederick Brokaw and Annie Doyle, I believed that we could do no less.

Central to my life's work has been to bring diverse people together, and so I include in this narrative the words of Ted Perry, who wrote the screenplay of a film produced by the Southern Baptist Convention (other than Bill Moyers, I rarely quote a Southern Baptist). Urban legend has it that this was a speech given by Chief Seattle in 1854, but it was actually written for a film in the 1970s. The film tanked, but these words are magnificent and echo the words in the book of Job and those of my friend, Chris Moore:

> How can you buy or sell the sky? The warmth of the land? Every
> part of the earth is sacred. Every shining pine needle. Every sandy

shore. Every mist in the dark woods. Every clearing and every humming insect is holy.

We are part of the earth and the earth is part of us. The perfumed flowers are our sisters. The deer, the horse, the great eagle. These are our brothers. The rocky crests. The juices in the meadow. The body heat of the pony. All belong to the same family. The rivers are our brothers. They quench our thirst. Remember—and teach your children.

All things are connected. . . . We did not weave the web of life. We are merely strands in it. Whatever we do to the earth, we do to ourselves. To harm the earth is to heap contempt on our Creator. We are part of the earth. It is part of us. Tell your children.[2]

At Intersections, we are fond of saying that we do our work at the thin places, but is there ever an occasion where the boundaries are thinner than at the transition between life and death? Than when each of us must confront our own mortality as we witness the passage from this life to the next of someone close to us? As George Eliot wrote, "Only in the agony of parting do we look into the depths of love."[3]

I am transfixed by those moments—transitions—between life and death, when we connect with eternal dimensions, when we lose ourselves in the wonder of the created universe, when we inhabit the ultimate of thin places. A rereading of John 14,[4] used so often in funeral services, prompts me to consider the place of miracles in our time—a time when science and technology so influence our daily patterns, when blockbuster movies so cloud our judgment about reality that we are almost conditioned to expect miracles to be accompanied by fire and brimstone, with scientific anomalies and extravagant special effects.

And yet, it is in those moments that set the context for John 14 that we really experience the miraculous: Friends and family accompanying one another through transitions, witnessing to faithfulness despite what seems to be all evidence to the contrary, finding hope and solace in God's continuing care—and in the love of a supportive community.

Perhaps, it is imagination that is key—that human quality that moves us to dare to dream, that emboldens us, that dimension of our heart and mind and soul that, when coupled with faith, moves us to ever deeper understandings of ourselves and our God. Imagination.

What one senses in the moment before death is on one side of the comma. It is all that is known and familiar. Despite the trials of this life, it is safe and predictable, but beyond the comma, we look for words and phrases, sentences, paragraphs and chapters still to be. Of all the things for which the human spirit yearns, it most needs hope, the possibility that there is a future beyond the endings of today, that there is a healing beyond the pain of the present, that there is something beyond the tears and darkness of a broken world. To offer a glimpse of these questions has been my life's work—I leave the pursuit of answers to my readers.

In this regard, I find one of the most powerful witnesses not in a futuristic communications expert, or some Internet guru, or a cutting edge film director, but in the words of a freed slave. In 1773, Phyllis Wheatley became the first African American author published in North America.[5] For those who have ears, may you hear Phillis Wheatley's poem "On Imagination" and understand why it is so important that we write the vision, and make it plain.

Imagination! Who can sing thy force?
Or who describe the swiftness of thy course?
Soaring through the air to find the bright abode
Th'empyreal palace of the thund'ring God
We on thy pinions can surpass the wind
And leave the rolling universe behind:
From star to star the mental optics rove,
Measure the skies, and range the realms above.

There in one view we grasp the mighty whole,
Or with new worlds amaze th'unbounded soul.[6]

As a storyteller, I began this narrative with an intersection of my internalized struggle about wearing glasses with the profound global reality of the Vietnam era that continues to impact our politics and our policies deep into the next century. I conclude with a similar intersection. There is a magnificent mosque in Astana, the capital city of Kazakhstan, where my Intersections colleague Farid Johnson and I were attending the World Forum of Spiritual Culture, a global conference of religious and cultural leaders dedicated to exploring religious and cultural vehicles in the pursuit of peace among nations.

The mosque's architecture is both delicate and massive. We had a break in the schedule and Farid and I visited the mosque—a huge facility in white and blue and gold—reminiscent of Wedgewood in its style—clean and crisp. There was almost no one in the mosque as Farid and I sat on prayer rugs and absorbed the stillness in the vast room.

He asked if he could pray for me. He did, in Arabic. It was one of the holiest moments in my life as this man from another faith and a vastly different life experience, and in a language I could not understand, offered thoughts to God about . . . me. I have never asked him what he prayed; I don't need to know. The experience was not one you could rationally explain, but the experience was . . . eternal.

Notes

PROLOGUE

1. Robert Fulghum, *All I Really Need to Know I Learned in Kindergarten* (New York: Random House, 1989), 80.

2. I am a preacher by vocation, and it is my practice to season images, illustrations, and reflections with passages, directly or implicitly, from Scripture. For those so inclined, pursuing these footnoted passages can lead to a richer and deeper understanding of the narrative I have written. The phrase here echoes the passage in Ephesians 3:20–21, "Now to him who by the power at work within us is able to accomplish abundantly far more than all we can ask or imagine, to him be glory in the church and in Christ Jesus to all generations, forever and ever. Amen." Unless otherwise noted, all biblical references are the New Revised Standard Version.

3. Using Disneyland as a metaphor for life itself, we can cite the words on a plaque there that say, "As long as there is imagination left in the world, Disneyland will never be complete." As memories propel us forward and imagination undergirds our continued efforts, we can find new and deeper purpose in our lives.

4. Muriel Rukeyser, *The Speed of Darkness* (New York: Random House, 1968).

5. Martin Luther King Jr., "Remaining Awake through a Great Revolution," commencement address, Oberlin College, Oberlin, Ohio, June 1965, http://www.oberlin.edu/external/EOG/BlackHistoryMonth/MLK/Comm Address.html.

6. Preached in the early years of the twenty-first century by Rev. Laurie Hafner, minister of Pilgrim United Church of Christ in Cleveland.

CHAPTER 1: GRATITUDE

1. e.e. cummings, "i thank You God for most this amazing," *Complete Poems, 1904–1962*, ed. George J. Firmage (New York: Grove Press, 1994), 663.

2. For an elaboration upon the use of the comma, see chapter 4.

CHAPTER 2: EVER NEW

1. Michael Strawser, *Both/And: Reading Kierkegaard from Irony to Edification* (New York: Fordham University Press, 1997), 17.

2. In Isaiah 43:16–19, we read:

> Thus says the LORD,
> who makes a way in the sea,
> a path in the mighty waters,
> [17]who brings out chariot and horse,
> army and warrior;
> they lie down, they cannot rise,
> they are extinguished, quenched like a wick:
> [18]Do not remember the former things,
> or consider the things of old.
> [19]I am about to do a new thing;
> now it springs forth, do you not perceive it?

CHAPTER 3: LISTENING

1. Natalie Goldberg, *Writing Down the Bones* (Boston: Shambala, 1986), 52–53.

2. Mrs Cecil Frances Alexander, "All Things Bright and Beautiful," 1848, http://www.telegraph.co.uk/culture/music/3668059/The-story-behind-the-hymn.html.

3. From *Network*, 1976 MGM, directed by Sydney Lumet, script by Paddy Chayefsky, https://www.youtube.com/watch?v=ZwMVMbmQBug.

4. Frederick Beuchner, *Wishful Thinking: A Seeker's ABC* (New York: HarperOne, 1993), 118–19.

5. All quotes in this paragraph from Dr. Martin Luther King Jr.'s "I Have A Dream" speech delivered August 28, 1963, at the Lincoln Memorial, Washington, D.C.; see script of speech at http://www.analytictech.com/mb 021/mlk.htm.

CHAPTER 4: COMMAS

1. Gracie Allen, in her last letter to husband George Burns, as quoted in Peter B. Panagore, *Two Minutes for God: Quick Fixes for the Spirit* (New York: Simon and Schuster, 2007), 73.

2. Under the leadership of my colleague Ron Buford, the creative and energetic team included Randy Varcho, Cliff Aerie, and Megan Hoelle.

3. It is important to recognize that the vast majority of individuals are not featured in the media and yet they very much exist and their contributions to a just world are significant. While it is important to be responsive to the media and to include an awareness of the media's power in any social justice strategy, it is also important to affirm the notion that notoriety does not equate with value.

4. Believe Out Loud is an online community that empowers Christians to work for lesbian, gay, bisexual, transgender, and queer (LGBTQ) equality. A primary "pillar" in Intersections' programming, Believe Out Loud reaches an average of more than five million people per month and has become a leading platform in Christian faith and LGBTQ advocacy.

Participants in Believe Out Loud hold many distinct identities and together seek to create a world where all Christian churches welcome and
affirm LGBTQ people. Believe Out Loud provides a community where participants can access resources for their journeys and share their own stories
of Christian faith and LGBTQ advocacy. Rooted in a framework of justice,
Believe Out Loud affirms members in these varied identities and challenges
LGBTQ Christians to "go and do likewise" (Luke 10:37). Believe Out Loud
was formed in 2009 and continues to be a program priority of Intersections.

5. The United Church of Canada's *Observer* magazine ran a long story
about the UCC entitled "The Church That Sold Itself Without Selling Its
Soul." There was a ten-fold increase in traffic on the denomination's website.
Three quarters of a million people went to the find-a-church functions on
UCC websites. People in prison and people on death's door contacted UCC
pastors because of this exposure. Thousands of e-mails were received in the
national offices in Cleveland. A church in Chapel Hill, North Carolina, had
fifty visitors the first Sunday the commercials ran; a congregation in Massachusetts registered sixty-seven visitors in the first month; a congregation in
Iowa saw forty new families; in Seminole, Florida, attendance at Christmas
Eve service increased by two hundred over the previous year, and doubled
the attendance at Easter. A small church in western Pennsylvania had fifty
people in attendance the last Sunday of November and ninety on the first
Sunday of December, once the commercial controversy became public. Another church in Iowa had less than one hundred people in worship in 2004
and five hundred less than two years later.

Yes, December 2004 set off an unprecedented explosion in UCC
recognition. Remember, this was the same church that only recently had
clamored for an identity campaign because its members felt invisible on
the world stage. My pastor at the time, Rev. Laurie Hafner, tells the story
of how her mom was one of the first to buy and wear a God Is Still Speaking T-shirt—long before the commercial controversy. When she wore her
shirt to the mall, people would come up to her and say, "Oh, what an interesting T-shirt." After the controversy, people would point to her T-shirt

and exclaim, "Oh, UCC!" Said Laurie's Mom, "I have been waiting my whole life for this."

6. Former President Obama's farewell remarks, Andrews Air Force Base, Maryland, January 20, 2017.

7. J. R. R. Tolkien, *The Hobbit*, chapter 12, "Inside Information" (New York: Ballantine Books, 1982), 217.

8. e.e. cummings, "since feeling is first," *Complete Poems, 1904–1962*, ed. George J. Firmage (New York: Grove Press, 1994), 291.

9. Oscar Wilde, *Lady Windemere's Fan*, 1892, act III.

CHAPTER 5: FAITH AND DOUBT

1. Anne Lamott, *Traveling Mercies: Some Thoughts on Faith* (New York, Random House,1999), 3.

2. John 20:19–29: When it was evening on that day, the first day of the week, and the doors of the house where the disciples had met were locked for fear of the Jews, Jesus came and stood among them and said, "Peace be with you." [20]After he said this, he showed them his hands and his side. Then the disciples rejoiced when they saw the Lord. [21]Jesus said to them again, "Peace be with you. As the Father has sent me, so I send you." [22]When he had said this, he breathed on them and said to them, "Receive the Holy Spirit. [23]If you forgive the sins of any, they are forgiven them; if you retain the sins of any, they are retained."

[24]But Thomas (who was called the Twin), one of the twelve, was not with them when Jesus came. [25]So the other disciples told him, "We have seen the Lord." But he said to them, "Unless I see the mark of the nails in his hands, and put my finger in the mark of the nails and my hand in his side, I will not believe."

[26]A week later his disciples were again in the house, and Thomas was with them. Although the doors were shut, Jesus came and stood among them and said, "Peace be with you." [27]Then he said to Thomas, "Put your finger here and see my hands. Reach out your hand and put it in my side. Do not doubt but believe." [28]Thomas answered him, "My Lord and my

God!" [29]Jesus said to him, "Have you believed because you have seen me? Blessed are those who have not seen and yet have come to believe."

3. Paul Tillich, *Systematic Theology, Volume II* (Chicago: University of Chicago Press, 1957), 116.

4. Arthur Turnbull, *The Life and Writings of Alfred Lord Tennyson* (London: Walter Scott, 1914), 185.

5. Harry Emerson Fosdick, "Doubting Your Doubts," in Thomas G. Long and Cornelius Platinga Jr., ed., *A Chorus of Witnesses: Model Sermons for Today's Preachers* (Grand Rapids, MI: Eerdmans; 1994), 110–19.

6. Paul Simon, "Proof," ©1990, *The Rhythm of the Saints*, http://www.paulsimon.com/track/proof-3/.

7. Frederick Buechner, *Beyond Words: Daily Readings in the ABC's of Faith* (New York: Harper Collins, 2004), 85.

8. Harry Emerson Fosdick, *The Meaning of Faith* (New York: Association Press, 1918), 195.

9. Peter Drucker, https://www.goodreads.com/author/quotes/12008.Peter _F_Drucker.

10. Note also that this passage, as quoted, ends with a comma.

CHAPTER 6: THE OTHER

1. Joan Baez, written in the sleeve notes for *Farewell, Angelina*, Vanguard, 1987.

2. This unprecedented initiative was part of a larger effort called the US-Pakistan Leaders Forum that brought together Americans and Pakistanis from a variety of civil society sectors to build relationships, alter stereotypes, and develop action agendas that promote mutual respect and understanding between both countries. The fourteen-member US-Pakistan Interreligious Consortium (UPIC) delegation was organized by Intersections in partnership with two prestigious universities in Pakistan—Lahore University of Management Sciences (LUMS) and the International Islamic University in Islamabad (IIU). This partnership was later joined by another Pakistani institution, the University of Management and Technology in Lahore. Our

visit in 2013 was our second trip to Pakistan, following an initial gathering in Oman.

3. Omar C. Garcia, Bible Teaching Notes, "Beliefs Held by Americans in Regard to the Bible," citing 1997 Barna Research Online, http://www.bible teachingnotes.com/templates/System/details.asp?id=29183&fetch=7872.

4. Index Mundi, "Pakistan Demographics Profile 2016," source: CIA World Factbook, http://www.indexmundi.com/pakistan/demographics_profile.html; some surveys place the number as high as 63%; see Friedrich Ebert Stiftung Office Pakistan, http://www.fes-pakistan.org/media/pdf/soccem _for_website-pdf.pdf.

5. Set in a broader context, Dr. Yasinzai's remarks are all the more revealing:

> While the diplomats, politicians and policymakers have their own ways of sorting out the differences in perspectives and positions on certain issues of what they like to call geostrategic concerns, the role of religious and grassroots leaders, I believe, is to examine the deeper aspects of these relationships—the aspects that bind the people of our two countries in our shared values. Whether we are Muslims, Christians, or Jews, whether we are Pakistanis or Americans, we all want to make this world a better place—more peaceful, more equitable, more responsive to the demands of justice and fairness, more tolerant and compassionate, and above all, based on morally informed and not on politically expedient policies. . . . Religious leaders speak from the pulpit of conscience and not from the soapbox of politicians. Hence, they have much more credibility than their counterparts in other sectors of society when they speak on issues of public interest, whether domestic or foreign.

6. These included Hofstra University, Georgetown University, Seton Hall University, and Christian Theological Seminary on the U.S. side, and LUMS, IIU, the University of Management and Technology (UMT), Edwardes College, and Forman Christian College in Pakistan.

7. According to the Institute of International Education, in 2014 there were more than 38,000 U.S. students studying in the United Kingdom, more than 10,000 in Germany, almost 6,000 in Japan, and yet, in Pakistan, there were only six; see http://www.iie.org/Research-and-Publications/Open-Doors/Data/US-Study-Abroad/All-Destinations/2012-14.

8. Upon returning from our trip in 2013, we received an e-mail from Dr. Mumtaz Ahmad, who wrote, "What really surprised—and pleasantly, at that—many of [my colleagues] here was the modesty and humility they saw in their American guests. It was surprising for them for two reasons: they often find their own religious leaders here mostly stiff-necked and self-righteous; and they thought that all Americans speak like the U.S. officials who visit Pakistan: 'We expect you to do more; we want you to become good boys.' Almost everyone told me that they saw a new face of America: deeply religious, caring, compassionate, humble, and willing to listen with respect and patience. You simply can't imagine, my friends, how important was your trip to Pakistan! It was for the first time that many of us came to know that 'winning hearts and minds' meant something real."

9. Ammara Mohsin, "Rising above Borders," *Discovery and Progress*, vol.7, issue 1 (September 15, 2014), KidSpirit Online, https://kidspiritonline.com/magazine/discovery-and-progress/rising-above-borders/, used by permission.

10. Ibid.

11. Much later, I became familiar with Stendahl's three rules of religious understanding, which he presented in a 1985 press conference in Stockholm, Sweden. His rules:

1. When you are trying to understand another religion, you should ask the adherents of that religion and not its enemies.
2. Don't compare your best to their worst.
3. Leave room for "holy envy." (By this Stendahl meant that you should be willing to recognize elements in the other religious tradition or faith that you admire and wish could, in some way, be reflected in your own religious tradition or faith.)

The wisdom of these guidelines became increasingly clear to me as I navigated the choppy seas of interreligious cooperation.

CHAPTER 7: SACRIFICE

1. William Butler Yeats, "The Stolen Child," published in 1889 in *The Wanderings of Oisin and Other Poems* (London: Kegan Paul and Co.).

2. Charles Dickens, *A Tale of Two Cities* (London: James Nisbet and Co., 1902), 3.

3. Ibid., 454.

4. Alain Boubil and Claude-Michel Schonberg, lyrics by Herbert Kretzmer, *Les Miserables*, Music Theatre International, 2011, 24.

5. ILIAC is an acronym created by Dr. Sidney B. Simon, professor of education, retired from the University of Massachusetts. His activity, I Am Lovable And Capable, was developed to help children not put themselves down and learn to value themselves. He later wrote a book by that title. The activity has become so popular that so many people have "borrowed" it (read "plagiarized") that they've separated his name and authorship from the material. He is still actively conducting trainings all over the United States. Because the metaphor in the exercise is a sign with the IALAC letters on it, people say, "He ripped my sign" when they mean "he hurt my feelings." See also http://www.urbandictionary.com/define.php ?term=IALAC.

6. "Overland Park Jewish Community Center Shooting," https://en .wikipedia.org/wiki/Overland_Park_Jewish_Community_Center_shooting.

7. On April 19, 2014, Yahoo News reported, "The leaflets were handed out by balaclava-clad men holding the flag of the Russian Federation earlier this week in the eastern city of Donetsk, and plastered to the walls of a synagogue. They ordered all Jewish citizens over 16 years old to register with the 'Donetsk Republic commissar for nationality affairs,' and pay a $50 fee. Those who refuse to register will be deprived of citizenship and forcibly expelled from the republic and their property will be confiscated," https://www.yahoo.com/news/ukraine-leaflets-calling-jewish-registration-

were-faked-140251712.html?ref=gs. See also Fox News, "US Jewish leaders deeply troubled by 'outrageous' pamphlets in Ukraine," http://www.foxnews .com/us/2014/04/18/us-jewish-leaders-deeply-troubled-by-anti-semitic-pamphlets-in-ukraine.html.

CHAPTER 8: RISK

1. Quote is widely attributed to Mahatma Gandhi.

2. Job, who lives a devout and faithful life, is struck by a series of tragedies caused by events beyond his control. His faith is severely challenged as he tries to make sense of how a merciful God could punish him so relentlessly despite his faithfulness. His friends try to get him to denounce God as being unjust, but Job refuses.

3. Luke 9:37–42:

> [37]On the next day, when they had come down from the mountain, a great crowd met him. [38]Just then a man from the crowd shouted, "Teacher, I beg you to look at my son; he is my only child. [39]Suddenly a spirit seizes him, and all at once he shrieks. It convulses him until he foams at the mouth; it mauls him and will scarcely leave him. [40]I begged your disciples to cast it out, but they could not." [41]Jesus answered, "You faithless and perverse generation, how much longer must I be with you and bear with you? Bring your son here." [42]While he was coming, the demon dashed him to the ground in convulsions. But Jesus rebuked the unclean spirit, healed the boy, and gave him back to his father.

4. See UCC's Sermon Seeds, February 9, 2013: Daniel Hazard, "Astounding Glory/Wholly Holy," reflection by Kate Huey, http://www.ucc.org /feed-your-spirit_weekly-seeds_astounding-glorywholly-holy.

5. As quoted in Sermon Seeds, Hazard, "Astounding Glory/Wholly Holy."

6. And yet, to this day, suspicions about Wes Diggs linger, as expressed in an article in the Bergen Record on the fortieth anniversary of the tragedy.

See http://www.northjersey.com/news/who-killed-the-diggs-family-40-year-old-mass-murder-in-teaneck-remains-a-mystery-1.1468498.

7. Matthew 25:14–30 reads:

[14]"For it is as if a man, going on a journey, summoned his slaves and entrusted his property to them; [15]to one he gave five talents, to another two, to another one, to each according to his ability. Then he went away. [16]The one who had received the five talents went off at once and traded with them, and made five more talents. [17]In the same way, the one who had the two talents made two more talents. [18]But the one who had received the one talent went off and dug a hole in the ground and hid his master's money. [19]After a long time the master of those slaves came and settled accounts with them. [20]Then the one who had received the five talents came forward, bringing five more talents, saying, 'Master, you handed over to me five talents; see, I have made five more talents.' [21]His master said to him, 'Well done, good and trustworthy slave; you have been trustworthy in a few things, I will put you in charge of many things; enter into the joy of your master.' [22]And the one with the two talents also came forward, saying, 'Master, you handed over to me two talents; see, I have made two more talents.' [23]His master said to him, 'Well done, good and trustworthy slave; you have been trustworthy in a few things, I will put you in charge of many things; enter into the joy of your master.' [24]Then the one who had received the one talent also came forward, saying, 'Master, I knew that you were a harsh man, reaping where you did not sow, and gathering where you did not scatter seed; [25]so I was afraid, and I went and hid your talent in the ground. Here you have what is yours.' [26]But his master replied, 'You wicked and lazy slave! You knew, did you, that I reap where I did not sow, and gather where I did not scatter? [27]Then you ought to have invested my money with the bankers,

and on my return I would have received what was my own with interest. [28]So take the talent from him, and give it to the one with the ten talents. [29]For to all those who have, more will be given, and they will have an abundance; but from those who have nothing, even what they have will be taken away. [30]As for this worthless slave, throw him into the outer darkness, where there will be weeping and gnashing of teeth.'"

8. See also Wikipedia, "Parable of the talents or minas," https://en.wikipedia.org/wiki/Parable_of_the_talents_or_minas, where we read "A talent (Ancient Greek, ταλαντο"scale" and "balance") was a unit of weight of approximately 80 pounds (36 kg), and when used as a unit of money, was valued for that weight of silver. As a unit of currency, a talent was worth about 6,000 denarii. Since a denarius was the usual payment for a day's labour, the value of a talent was about twenty years of labour, by an ordinary person. By contemporary standards (ca. AD 2009) at the rate of the US minimum wage of $7.25 per hour, the value of a talent would be approximately $300,000 over 20 years, while, at the median yearly wage of $26,363, a talent would be valued at about $500,000; source William Ridgeway, "Measures and Weights, in Leonard Whibley, ed. *A Companion to Greek Studies* (Cambridge, UK: Cambridge University Press, 1905), 444.

9. Chris Haslam, "Comments: Revised Common Lectionary: Clippings: Twenty-third Sunday after Pentecost, November 16, 2014," Christ Church Cathedral website, http://montreal.anglican.org/comments/archive/apr33l .shtml; see commentary on Matthew 25:14–30, verse 21.

10. John Wesley, *Explanatory Notes upon the New Testament* (New York: Lane and Scott, 1850), 84.

11. William Loader, "First Thoughts on Passages from Matthew in the Lectionary: Pentecost 23," http://wwwstaff.murdoch.edu.au/~loader/Mt-Pentecost23.htm.

CHAPTER 9: ART AND CULTURE

1. Quoted in Sergei Eisenstein, *The Film Sense*, ed. and tranl. Jay Leyda (New York: Meridian Books, 1957), 127; from an apocryphal letter published originally in Ogoniok (Moscow), May 16, 1926, https://rosswolfe.files.wordpress.com/2015/03/sergei-eisenstein-film-sense.pdf.

2. Madeleine L'Engle, *Walking on Water: Reflections on Faith and Art* (New York: North Point Press, 1980), 134.

3. Sarah Klassen, "Faith, Art, and Reconciliation," *Direction* vol.27, no. 2 (fall 1998), 101–8, http://www.directionjournal.org/27/2/faith-art-and-reconciliation.html.

4. Michael Edwards, *Toward a Christian Poetics* (New York: Macmillan, 1984), 73f.

5. Robert Wuthnow, *Creative Spirituality: The Way of the Artist* (Berkely: University of California Press, 2001), 9.

6. W. C. McGrew, *Primates and the Origin of Culture* (Cambridge, UK: University of Cambridge, 2007).

CHAPTER 10: GENERATIONS

1. Antoine de Saint-Exupery's *The Little Prince*, published posthumously in France in 1943, is among the top four selling books in the world and has been translated into more than 250 languages and dialects.

2. Ray Kurzweil, *The Age of Spiritual Machines* (New York: Viking, 1999), 36–37.

3. Ibid, 37.

CHAPTER 11: KEEP TALKING

1. Stephen R. Covey, *The 7 Habits of Highly Effective People: Powerful Lessons in Personal Change* (New York: Free Press, 1989), 238.

2. See the Arms Control Association's "Timeline of Syrian Chemical Weapons Activity, 2012–2016, October 2016, https://www.armscontrol.org/factsheets/Timeline-of-Syrian-Chemical-Weapons-Activity; Glenn Kessler, "President Obama and the 'red line' on Syria's chemical weapons," *Wash-*

ington Post, September 6, 2013, https://www.washingtonpost.com/news
/fact-checker/wp/2013/09/06/president-obama-and-the-red-line-on-syrias-
chemical-weapons/; Ruth Sherlock, "Syria chemical weapons: the roof that
Assad regime launching chlorine attacks on children," April 29, 2014, http://
www.telegraph.co.uk/news/worldnews/middleeast/syria/10796175/Syria-
chemical-weapons-the-proof-that-Assad-regime-launching-chlorine-at-
tacks-on-children.html.

CHAPTER 12: INTERSECTIONS

1. Krista Tippett, host of *On Being,* a syndicated public radio program
and podcast.

2. Bruce Lawrence, "Youtube Terrorism," Religion Dispatches, September
12, 2012, http://religiondispatches.org/youtube-terrorism/#disqus_thread.

3. See Peter Bregman, "Diversity Training Doesn't Work," March 12,
2012, Harvard Business Review, https://hbr.org/2012/03/diversity-training-
doesnt-work.

CHAPTER 13: RACE

1. Ta-Nehisi Coates, author of *Between the World and Me,* during an interview on NPR, July 10, 2015.

2. The others are changing water to wine (John 2:1–12); healing of the
official's son (John 4:43–54); healing a paralyzed man (John 5:1–15); feed-
ing the five thousand (John 6:1–15); walking on water (John 6:16–24); and
healing a man born blind (John 9:1–12).

3. Despite right-wing rhetoric, the affirmation that black lives matter is
not a contradiction to the notion that blue lives matter. This is a false di-
chotomy, set up by those who seek to ignore the impact of systemic racism
on people of color. #BlackLivesMatter is a recognition that, too often in our
society, the systems that support our way of life have responded as if people
of color are invisible, are voiceless, and have less intrinsic value. This movement affirms the opposite: that people of color have the same rights, re-

sponsibilities, and human potential as those within the dominant culture. In words from the #BlackLivesMatter website, "BlackLivesMatter is working for a world where Black lives are no longer systematically and intentionally targeted for demise. We affirm our contributions to this society, our humanity, and our resilience in the face of deadly oppression. We have put our sweat equity and love for Black people into creating a political project— taking the hashtag off of social media and into the streets. The call for Black lives to matter is a rallying cry for ALL Black lives striving for liberation." See also http://blacklivesmatter.com/who-we-are/.

4. Kimbriel Kelly and Wesley Lowery, "Cleveland officer acquitted in killing of unarmed pair amid barrage of gunfire," *Washington Post,* May 23, 2015, https://www.washingtonpost.com/investigations/cleveland-police-officer-found-not-guilty-in-fatal-shooting-of-two-people/2015/05/23/280844f0-f028-11e4-a55f-38924fca94f9_story.html.

5. See Aisha Tyler, "As It Happened: A timeline of the Emanuel AME Church shooting," June 17, 2016, http://www.live5news.com/story/32227023/as-it-happened-a-timeline-of-the-emanuel-ame-church-shooting; also http://time.com/time-magazine-charleston-shooting-cover-story/.

CHAPTER 14: TRUTH

1. Maya Angelou, "Still I Rise," from her third volume of poetry, *And Still I Rise: A Book of Poems* (New York: Random House, 1978).

2. Robert Chase, *Diggs* (New York: Vantage Press, 1981), 74–75.

3. As of this writing, a recent mass shooting—the deadliest in American history—occurred at the LGBTQ nightclub Pulse in Orlando, Florida. See Ariel Zambelich and Alyson Hurt, "3 Hours in Orlando: Piecing Together an Attack and Its Aftermath," June 26, 1016, http://www.npr.org/2016/06/16/482322488/orlando-shooting-what-happened-update; see also the National Association of Social Workers' blog "NASW Response to Orlando Massacre: Sensible Gun Laws, Treat Gun Violence as a Public Health Threat, and End Culture of Hatred," http://www.socialworkblog.org/advocacy/2016/06

/nasw-response-to-orlando-massacre-sensible-gun-laws-treat-gun-violence-as-a-public-health-threat-and-end-culture-of-hate/, for treating gun violence as a public health issue.

4. John C. Holbert, "The Righteous and Their Faithfulness: Reflections on Habakkuk 1:1–4; 2:1–4," October 27, 2013, Patheos, http://www.patheos.com/Progressive-Christian/Righteous-Faithfulness-John-Holbert-10-28-2013.

CHAPTER 15: FORGIVENESS

1. The quote has been widely attributed to Mark Twain, American writer, born Samuel Langhorne Clemens in 1835, but may have older origins, according to Quote Investigator, http://quoteinvestigator.com/2013/09/30/violet-forgive/.

2. Cleophus LaRue, "It Will Surely Come," program 4517, February 3, 2002, http://www.30goodminutes.org/index.php/archives/23-member-archives/453-cleophus-larue-program-4517.

3. David Ewart, Holy Textures.com, "Matthew 9:9–13, 18–26," http://www.holytextures.com/Matthew-09-09-13-18-26.pdf.

CHAPTER 16: 9/11 RIBBONS

1. In consoling White House and Congressional staff members on the occasion of Donald Trump's winning the 2016 presidential election, as reported by Julie Herschfeld Davis, "After Election, Commander in Chief Soothes White House Workers," *New York Times*, November 11, 2016, A12; https://www.nytimes.com/2016/11/12/us/politics/obama-west-wing.html.

2. Chris Moore, Landmarks Commission meeting remarks, used by permission. The full text of his remarks is as follows:

> I had just come out of the World Trade Center subway station at Chambers and Church Street when it happened. . . . None of us knew that the fireball we saw rise up the tower had been

caused by a plane crash. From my angle I could not see a plane hitting the tower, only the huge ball of fire.

I had just come out of the subway, to hear an explosion and a loud gasp from people on Church Street. I looked up to see the fire climbing the tower. Somebody yelled it was a bomb. But pieces were shooting out of the building and spraying down toward us. I didn't know it was a plane engine, a tire, and the landing gear.

I had no idea what I was witnessing. I thought a movie was being made. And I thought it was being made dangerously close to the public. . . . I heard someone say in a tone of absolute disbelief, "People are jumping from the building." As I heard it, I saw two people falling down the building. If I hadn't heard those words at the exact place that I was looking, I don't think I would have known what I was seeing. I knew it wasn't a movie . . .

Before I turned to leave, I looked up at both buildings and prayed for the lives of the people I had seen die or dying, and for those many, many people who had already died, whom I just knew were going to die. That more people, emergency workers, firefighters, and police would actually enter those towers to save lives will never be lost to me. . . . For almost ten years now, whenever I am on the bridge or come out of the subway at Chambers Street, I find the place where the towers stood, and I think about 9/11, and I think about those people.

To the issue of designation as an individual landmark, Mr. Chair, I do not find the importance of 47 Park Place to be its architecture. . . . I do find significance to its connection to the events of September 11, 2001. . . . Whether the cast iron rusts and falls apart, or whether it is replaced by the most famous community center in the world, or a church, its space will always memorialize the people who were in those planes, and in those buildings, and in the sky. Last I looked, we do not landmark the sky . . . I do not support the designation.

3. View the video *We the People* at http://www.intersections.org/video-gallery?page=5.

4. Kevin Jones, "Shadows," in the video *Shadows,* Prepare New York, 2011, http://www.intersections.org/video-gallery?page=4.

CHAPTER 17: ANCESTORS

1. T. S. Eliot, "East Coker," first published in 1940 in *New English Weekly*, then in *Four Quartets* (New York: Harcourt, 1943).

2. "The IUCN Red List of Threatened Species," http://www.iucnredlist.org/initiatives/mammals/analysis/red-list-status.

3. "The Extinction Crisis," Center for Biological Diversity, http://www.biologicaldiversity.org/programs/biodiversity/elements_of_biodiversity/extinction_crisis/.

4. Alister Doyle, "Ice bridge holding Antarctic ice shelf cracks up," April 6, 2009, Reuters Science News, http://www.reuters.com/article/us-antarctica-ice-idUSTRE5326HO20090406.

5. Suzanne Goldberg, "Arctic sea ice extent breaks record low for winter," *The Guardian,* March 28, 2016, https://www.theguardian.com/environment/2016/mar/28/arctic-sea-ice-record-low-winter.

6. Genesis 1:26: Then God said, "Let us make humankind in our image, according to our likeness; *and let them have dominion* [italics mine] over the fish of the sea, and over the birds of the air, and over the cattle, and over all the wild animals of the earth, and over every creeping thing that creeps upon the earth."

7. Lynn White, Jr.'s "The Historical Roots of Our Ecological Crisis," 1967, http://www.zbi.ee/~kalevi/lwhite.htm, became perhaps the most widely cited article within theological debate about ecology; see "Is Christianity to Blame?" University of Exeter, http://humanities.exeter.ac.uk/theology/research/projects/beyondstewardship/blame/#Article.

8. William Golding, *The Inheritors* (London: Faber and Faber, 1955).

9. ICMN staff, "President Obama Releases National Native American Heritage Month Proclamation," November 2, 2012, Indian Country Media

Network, http://indiancountrytodaymedianetwork.com/2012/11/01/president-obama-releases-national-native-american-heritage-month-proclamation-143524.

10. Arleen Richards, "Debunking the Myth of the Manhattan Purchase," *Epoch Times,* November 14, 2014.

11. James Barron, "The Sale of Manhattan, Retold from a Native American Viewpoint," November 18, 2014, http://www.nytimes.com/2014/11/19/arts/music/the-sale-of-manhattan-retold-from-a-native-american-viewpoint.html?_r=0.

12. Bernice Elizabeth Green, "Project Re-education Lenape's Griot Voices: Of Truth They Sing Part 1 of 3: 'Purchase of Manhattan,' An Opera About Justice, Forgiveness, Healing, Returning Home and More" *Our Time Press*, November 14, 2014.

13. Antonia Blumberg, "'Purchase of Manhattan' Opera Aims to Heal a 400-year-old Wound," November 17, 2014, http://www.huffingtonpost.com/2014/11/17/purchase-of-manhattan_n_6135062.html.

14. Ibid.

15. Richards, "Debunking the Myth of the Manhattan Purchase."

CHAPTER 18: BALANCE

1. Paul Simon, "Old Friends," from the album *Bookends*, 1968, Columbia Records.

2. Phil Klay, "After War: A Failure of the Imagination," *New York Times*, February 8, 2014.

3. Tina's story, used with her permission:

Dear Bob,

Thank you for sending this latest news. I'm so very glad that you made it through the gauntlet; I know how scary it must have been for you and your family. I hope that my sharing is not too personal, but your "story" was so pure and such a clear retelling of all the feelings an injured person endures, that it re-opened my daily dialogue with myself, and I was literally driven to my keyboard.

First, I would say from how well written and articulate your writing is, you don't have anything to worry about! Second, honestly, you will never be the same; you will be better, bigger, brighter. Ain't life grand?

I had a stroke in 2005, and, yes, it is, on a very visceral, personal, internalized level, a life-changing event. Sounds trite, but it's true. I was unable to explain it to anyone clearly. It took me many months to finally unearth the one word that could describe the reality of how I felt: vulnerable.

I was unequipped to communicate with the world about my post-stroke life. I was considered very, very lucky (and therefore trapped in a no-complaints-allowed haze), in that all my physical abilities "popped back" within 28 hours: like a thunder strike from the beyond, my brain rebooted my body. Electric charges, sizzling sounds, and I was back! Sort of. What I discovered was that nothing was the same, except my reflection. And that in itself was confusing. It was a lot of "you look fine, totally, so what's the problem?" or "You didn't really have a stroke . . . really? I'd never know . . ." But I knew those closest to me saw and felt "the change." I certainly did. I thought, "I've been rendered stupid" as I sat and stared at my socks, trying to determine just what I was supposed to do with them. I was back at work a few weeks after as if nothing had happened, yet I didn't drive a car for 9 months (my own decision). I wandered the aisles of the grocery store in paranoia (a new feeling for me) worrying about my choices (food labels were complex).

Crowds were scary; heck, stairs were scary! Sequencing was my biggest problem: using your phrase, connecting the dots, now seemed like a lost cause. I agonized over whether I was ever coming back with full-steam. . . . I wanted my old self back. It took a long time, but inch by inch I noticed more and more that my brain felt "normal" again. I recognized myself! I had more better days than bad ones. I learned how to selfishly take better care of me: eating, sleeping, resting. Sometimes still I "get up on the wrong side of the bed" and within minutes I know I'm not quite right, so I lie down for 20 more minutes in a dream sleep state, and when I next get up, I'm fine. I learned to listen more to myself and others, and I slowed myself down quite a bit; I was happy to hear that the latest research shows that being a star multitasker isn't everything it was cracked up to be. I have come to like my new self: more focused, more present, interested, and always in the moment. (Maybe I wasn't as smart as I thought I was to begin with!)

It has now been over 8 years and I can switch the blame for any inaccuracies and memory voids on simple aging. Ahhh, finally a reward for being a 50-something! And luckily, my friends and family are a loving bunch, and I have a diverse and busy job working with an incredibly kind, understanding man, who in his 70s is the epitome of energy, vitality, and forward-thinking. He sets a very high bar! (When describing me to others, he typically says, "Ask the Chief; I'm just a sax player!")

But what your recent writings say to me, is not to be shut down. Don't file it away and forget about it; instead let all the people around you know. I didn't think there was much anymore to dwell on surrounding my medical event, and lately whenever I tell someone that once upon a time I had a stroke, I wonder if I'm groping for a convenient excuse for my short-comings, using it like a crutch, rehashing old news, squeezing out the last drops of sympathy ("Maybe they'll cut me some slack") but then I stop and think: why would I want to forget about such an impactful, life-changing event? Any shame has morphed into pride; my stroke is now part of who I am, another chapter in my life, and as long as I'm willing to share my experience, a chapter in every-

one else's life, too. You have brought me to a deeper understanding that what's really important is the shared experience. It's not
the forgetting; it's the remembering. Sharing allows everyone to
understand. It empowers all of us. It removes fear from both the
storyteller and the listener. I understand now the wisdom in embracing these "accidents." You have seized the opportunity to ed-
ucate and enlighten the rest of us; reminding us that we all have
value to add, and that we all enrich each other. The incontrovertible truth: "for every action there is a reaction"—and the surprise is that both have equal value.

I tell folks that I'm like a 500-piece puzzle, with just a few
pieces missing . . . not so bad! I think that you must be a 1000+
piece puzzle; stupendous! I'm so glad I got to meet you at Solstice
in the year of the "ribbons." And I thoroughly enjoy all of your
writings. . . . Keep 'em coming! All my best,

Christina
Christina Andersen, Coordinator
Paul Winter Consort, Earth Music Productions, LLC

CHAPTER 19: BEYOND DEATH

1. Charles Reznikoff, "If There Is a Scheme," from *The Complete Poems of Charles Reznikoff, 1918–1975* by Charles Reznikoff, ed. by Seamus Cooney (Boston: Black Sparrow Books, 2005), 107. Reprinted by permission.

2. Ted Perry, film script for *Home* (prod. by the Southern Baptist Radio and Television Commission, 1972), reprinted in Rudolf Kaiser, "Chief Seat-tle's Speech(es): American Origins and European Reception," in *Recovering the Word: Essays on Native American Literature*, ed. Brian Swann and Arnold Krupat (Berkeley: University of California Press, 1987), 525–30, http://www.washington.edu/uwired/outreach/cspn/Website/Classroom%20Materials/Reading%20the%20Region/Texts%20by%20and%20about%20

Natives/Texts/8.html; see also Ann Medlock, "Chief Seattle's Screenwriter," *Huffington Post*, November 13, 2007, http://www.huffingtonpost.com /ann-medlock/chief-seattles-screenwrit_b_72510.html.

3. George Eliot, *Felix Holt, the Radical* (New York: Little, Brown, 1900), 428.

4. John 14:1–3: "Do not let your hearts be troubled. Believe in God, believe also in me. [2]In my Father's house there are many dwelling places. If it were not so, would I have told you that I go to prepare a place for you? [3]And if I go and prepare a place for you, I will come again and will take you to myself, so that where I am, there you may be also."

5. Wheatley was a member of Old South Congregational Church (now a UCC church in the heart of Boston).

6. Phyllis Wheatley (1753–84), "On Imagination," published in *Poems on Various Subjects* (London: A. Bell, 1773), http://www.bartleby.com /150/19.html.